PRAISE FOR PILGRIM WHEELS

"*Pilgrim Wheels* is a terrifically observed story of a bicycle journey. Neil Hanson captures perfectly what it's like to ride the open roads. The prose makes you feel brutal headwinds, unimaginable inclines, and the heat and dryness of the desert, where 'there's no instrument for the wind to play.' The small encounters, little epiphanies, kindnesses from strangers, and recollections make this story compelling and unique. This is *On the Road* meets *Zen and the Art of Motorcycle Maintenance*. The writing is superb. The book is filled with memorable characters and situations. The chapter epigraphs alone are worth the price of admission. Honestly, I couldn't put it down."

—**George O'Har**, author of *The Thousand Hour Club*

"Hanson takes the reader with him in a way few authors can. You feel the heat of the "sledgehammer sun" in the Sonoran desert, the hot wind blowing him across the Mojave. You feel the dogs nipping at his heels, and the steep climbs. You really feel that you meet the people he describes along the way."

—**Louis Frouws**, author of *The Cyclist's Mind Goes Everywhere*

"More than the story of a bicycle ride across America, Hanson relates himself to the culture, history and scenery, which weave together to form the magical moments we all seek. I've found a kindred spirit—a cyclosopher."

—**Scott Stoll**, author of *Falling Uphill*

PILGRIM WHEELS

Monterey, CA

PILGRIM WHEELS

Medicine Lodge, KS

REFLECTIONS OF A CYCLIST
CROSSING AMERICA
NEIL HANSON

HIGH PRAIRIE PRESS DENVER

HIGH PRAIRIE PRESS
6403 South Hudson Street
Centennial, CO 80121
www.highprairiepress.com
neil@neilhanson.com

Printed in the United States of America

First Printing, 2015

ISBN 978-0-9826391-2-2

Library of Congress Control Number: 2014917812

Speaking engagements and other author events scheduled through:
High Prairie Press
Neil Hanson
neil@neilhanson.com

Grateful acknowledgement is made to Emily Kachorek for permission to reprint the quotation in Chapter 25.

Editing by Erin Willard, www.erincopyeditor.com

Book design and illustrations by K.M.Weber, www.ilibribookdesign.com

We shall not cease from exploration
And the end of all our exploring
Will be to arrive where we started
And know the place for the first time.

T. S. Eliot, *Four Quartets*

ACKNOWLEDGMENTS

Dave Giesler is a great friend and fantastic traveling companion. The many hours, days, and weeks we've spent together on the road have been a great joy in my life. I'm thankful and grateful to have him as a friend in my life. As we completed half the miles of this journey together, he never complained about my dilly-dallying for photographs, and tolerated my whining about headwinds like the true friend he is. In addition, Dave read many versions of the story as it evolved, helping greatly in defining the end result.

Paula Margulies is my publicist, and continues to be a great help to me in learning the publicity side of the indie publishing business. Erin Willard edited the manuscript. She is a master at her craft, and I remain amazed at the many ways an editor can point out my mistakes while making me feel good about it.

Great journeys don't just happen. They require the support and love of those around us. Thanks to the folks in my life who were supportive and helpful as this journey became a reality. Thanks as well to those who have been so generous in providing excellent feedback to help the journey I took evolve into the story on these pages. Those most dear in my life have been loving and supportive throughout the journey, and I'm very grateful for that. Thank You!

Thanks to the many people who allowed me to include their words and quotations in the story. Those words often capture the moment far better than my words could have, and I am grateful for their generous spirit.

Finally, I'd like to thank you, the reader, for sharing this adventure with me. Words are instruments we play and listen to with our minds, and the words I use here have meaning and impact only when you, kind reader, choose to pick up my story and read it. Thank you.

INTRODUCTION

As I make my slow pilgrimage through the world, a certain sense of beautiful mystery seems to gather and grow.

A. C. Benson

Eric Clapton said once that we all see our lives as a pilgrimage of sorts, and that he saw his life as a pilgrimage to know himself. While I don't think most of us see our entire lives as a pilgrimage, I do think there are times, places, journeys, or events in our lives that we view as pilgrimages in some way. It could be a journey into some place of deep religious significance, a journey out through the woods for a time of re-creation, a quest toward some new land in search of adventure, or a transition into a new life.

A pilgrimage isn't necessarily *to* anything, and not necessarily *from* anything. In fact, I suspect the greatest pilgrimages don't start off as pilgrimages at all, but rather as something else. Possibly an adventure. Maybe a journey at just the right time in a person's life.

That's what this story is about. The idea of an adventure, that evolved into a journey, and from which a pilgrimage blossomed.

I wanted to take a bike ride. A long bike ride. Hundreds of miles, just me and my bike. Why? No particular reason, it just sounded like a neat thing to add to the checklist of "fun and exciting things I've tried." My friend Dave thought it would be a fun checklist item too. An adventure was conceived.

As we planned, the idea morphed, evolving eventually into a two-wheeled adventure from the west coast to the east coast. We didn't define the adventure as "we must go from coast to coast," but we both knew that by the time it was over, that's what would happen. It wouldn't be a single leg shared by both of us, but rather a couple different legs, dictated by the logistics of job situations. It turned out that, once it was complete, we'd ridden about half the miles together, and about half the miles alone.

So it began. An idea became an adventure. An adventure to plan for and to move toward. A box to check off. Eventually, I was clipping into my pedals in Monterey, California, pointing south along the coast on a beautiful summer day.

As I started turning those pedals, a new complexion began to take shape in the nature of this adventure. Out on the road, by myself, the *adventure* began to subside, as the *journey* began to grow. I was enveloped within the redwoods in Big Sur, and launched down the back side of the coastal range into the Central Valley wine country. By then, each pedal stroke felt like a step along the path of journey into something.

By the time I sailed out onto the Great American Desert of the Southwest, I felt the journey becoming deeper, quieter, brighter. Leaving Twentynine Palms in California, I was swept across a brightly burning Mojave Desert by a scorching desert wind, feeling the journey germinating into something unexpected. The sweet fragrance of pilgrimage surrounded me, sharpening my vision, tuning my ears to the wonder whispered in the silence around me. Before I'd passed out of the Sonoran, I was wrapped completely in the blossom of pilgrimage.

This is the story of that journey, and my reflections as I passed through it and it passed through me. Reflections of wonders along the path, obstacles faced, pain endured, and boundless joy discovered. Reflections about myself, the people I met, the land I traveled through, and the places that opened up to me. Joyful places, social places, quiet places and sacred places.

There's more to the journey than could be fit into one volume, both figuratively and literally. This volume takes the reader up to Kansas, and I can think of no better place to pause the narrative than the middle of Kansas. Dave and I swept down into Medicine Lodge in southwest Kansas on a glorious July day, after a morning of flying along the highway through the Medicine Hills. The Medicine Hills have been a place of wonder and magic for thousands of years for people who've lived there. A place made for pilgrims. A perfect place to pause the wheels and reflect.

This is a story of journey, discovery, and place, a song told from the saddle of my bicycle as I push and pull on the pedals, rolling down the highway. The crank turning round and round provides the rhythm while my bicycle chain hums the melody. The wind steps in with a harmony now and then, sometimes sweet as it pushes me down the road, sometimes dissonant in my face.

> *To ride a bicycle properly is very much like a love affair; chiefly it is a matter of faith. Believe you can do it and the thing is done; doubt, and for the life of you, you cannot.*
> H. G. Wells, *The Wheels of Chance*

PROLOGUE

*You are only afraid if you are not
in harmony with yourself.*

Hermann Hesse

MAY 28, 2011 · COLORADO

"My god, Neil, I never knew you were such a stud!"

The words catch me a bit off-guard. I mean, what guy doesn't want such a thing said about him? Of course, the fact that the person exclaiming this is a friend named Kyle, and not some gorgeous beauty, detracts from the value of the statement. Nonetheless, I'm a bit at a loss for words. How do you respond to something like that? I don't think I've ever had to think about it before.

I'm at a wedding reception dinner with a group of friends. They're acquaintances I've known from around my neighborhood for many years. We've been talking about summer plans, and I've shared that when I leave the dinner here in an hour or so, I'll be climbing into a rental car, driving the car out to Monterey in California, and riding my bike back through Colorado and east. A couple of jaws drop.

Kyle shakes his head in amazement. "Really, I can't believe this, Neil."

Okay, now my head's starting to swell. At the same time, I wonder if maybe I've bitten off more than I can chew. Doubt begins to float around in my little brain. I'm a pretty normal middle-aged guy, and this is just a bike ride. Climbing on the bike and pedaling. Anybody can do that. Right? It's a long ride for sure, long enough that not many folks would take it on, but still just riding a bike.

"So how many miles will it be?" Kyle continues with the attention.

"Well, by the time I get all the way across the country it will be 3,500 miles or so. The west coast to Kansas will about half of that."

"And how long is this going to take?"

"Around three weeks for the west coast to Kansas section, something close to forty days to cross the country."

Kyle shakes his head. "Man oh man." On the one hand it's nice to bask in this attention, but on the other hand I'm starting to feel uncomfortable—both with the attention and the doubts it's triggering in me.

Leaving dinner at six p.m., I change in the parking lot, trading my suit for a pair of worn-out throw-away jeans and t-shirt. Leaving the suit behind, I climb into the rental car with my bicycle. I'm feeling a sense of urgency to get on the road, partially motivated by the doubts that the recent conversation has created, but largely driven by my sense that I'm falling a little behind schedule. It's Saturday evening, and I need to be 1,500 miles from here on Monday, riding my bike back in this direction.

After a brief three-hour sleep in a little motel somewhere in New Mexico, I'm driving again with first light. It's morning, the sun's shining brightly in the world again, and my confidence strengthens with the sweet hope and optimism that morning brings.

I spend Sunday making my way deeper into the deserts

of the Southwest. By midday, it's clear to me that I'm doing fine on time and schedule. There's 100 miles of desert that I'll be riding through with no place to fill water bottles, so I drive that road to scout it. Finding a good spot to cache a gallon of water under a mesquite bush, I verify landmarks so I can find the water later before climbing back into the car and continuing west.

Pulling into the airport in Monterey the next afternoon, the doubts lurking around the edges of my mind have blossomed. Dread creeps in. For the past couple days, this rental car has been my "base camp" as I've traveled out here from Colorado, and I'm reluctant to give it up. I've driven a lot of miles to get here, and the many hours in the car have me wondering about whether I'm really up for backtracking those 1,500 miles on a bicycle, most of the way by myself.

Self-doubt is a powerful force. Any tiny crack in confidence invites that nasty self-doubt demon to find a way to slip between the conscious and the unconscious mind, creating havoc, inventing lists of things that might go wrong, dredging up past failures real or perceived.

I park the car in the rental lot, rigging my bike for riding. Forcing myself to move away from the car, I push my bike into the airport, where I drop off the keys at the Hertz counter. After changing from my driving clothes to my riding clothes in the men's room, I drop the old t-shirt and jeans into a trash can, giving the trash can one last glance over my shoulder as I make my way toward the doors that will take me out of the airport.

That simple gesture—dropping those clothes in the trash can—lifts a weight from my shoulders. It releases the last remaining connection to the security of the rental car. Behind me is the journey that brought me to this point. I turn back toward the doors that will take me out of the airport, forward, toward the journey in front of me.

Monterey, CA

Paso Robles, CA

BIG SUR

1

CARMEL, THE BEAUTIFUL PEOPLE

What we call the beginning is often the end. And to make an end is to make a beginning. The end is where we start from.

T. S. Elliot

DAY 1 · INTO CARMEL BY THE SEA, CALIFORNIA

The automatic doors part for me as I push my bicycle across the threshold into the bright Monterey sunlight. The safety and protection of a controlled and modern world is in back of me, shrouded in low light and a quiet hum. The bright light of adventure lay in front of me.

A pretty young woman sits on a bench outside the terminal. We catch each other's eye with small smiles a couple times. I think this is flirting, though I'm not very good at either recognizing it or executing it. I'm pretty logical, which drives me to want to analyze and evaluate things. With flirting, once you analyze it, the opportunity has passed.

There's a process, an unspoken ritual, that's wrapped around flirting. A little of this, a little of that, then maybe some of this over here. It's all body language and vibe. For folks like me who rely a lot on logic and words, with an analytical bent, flirting is unknown and confusing territory. I suck at it.

The young woman rescues the situation (I suspect it's usually the woman who must rescue any flirting situation if it's to progress) by offering the first comment:

"Did you bring that bike on the airplane?"

I smile. "Actually, I just dropped off a rental car. I brought the bike with me in the car."

"Are you here to visit?" she asks.

"Don't know a soul out here. I'm riding my bike across the country."

Her jaw drops and her eyes get wide. Now, if she were to exclaim that I must be some kind of stud, life would feel really sweet. I could ride down the road basking in the knowledge that a pretty young woman thinks I'm a stud.

My reaction here is different from my reaction back in Colorado. I'm already here, and I've dropped off the rental car. I'm pretty committed. Her reaction of astonishment doesn't sow doubt in my mind, but instead I feel something I haven't yet felt—a sense of commitment to the journey. It feels good. I can do this.

"How about you," I ask, "are you visiting friends?"

"I don't know a soul out here either. There's a writer's conference I'm attending down in Carmel this week. I'm trying to get started as a writer."

What a neat bit of synchronicity. I smile at the thought. She answers her phone and has a short conversation, obviously her boyfriend back home on the east coast, while I make some final adjustments to my gear.

She hangs up, and asks, "Do you have a camera? I could take your picture before you start your ride."

The picture she takes will speak volumes to me later. My white legs are lacking the dark tan the desert will soon burn into them, my face still bathed in a cockiness untempered by 12 percent climbs and desert dogs.

Her ride pulls up. Just before she closes the door, she looks back at me. We smile and give each other a knowing little upward jerk of the head. *Be well*, it says. *May the Force be with you. Live long and prosper.*

Watching her pull away, I feel an odd camaraderie with her. She, too, is embarking on an adventure in her life. I don't get her name, but it's the first of many connections I'll feel with folks along the way.

Here in the airport, surrounded by people and machines and noise, two people embark on separate adventures. We connect briefly, smile, and exchange a few words, each of us recognizing the pilgrim's heart in the other.

My ride over to Carmel gives me a taste of some climbing, and with it a little opportunity for worry. There's a sharp but small pain in one of my knees, leading me to wonder whether or not I've trained enough for the ride. Either I've trained enough, or I haven't, and at this point all I can do is gear down and take it easy, take a little pressure off the knee.

So I do. I gear down. As the sharp pain behind my knee subsides, worry drops behind me, leaking from my soul, leaving room for the joy of a beautiful afternoon to rush back in. Worry is such an expensive thing to accept. It's a black hole, into which enjoyment of the present moment plummets. Hard to recognize when it's sucking the joy from your soul, it's crystal clear once it passes through and departs.

Cresting the final climb, I smile and fall away into a wonderful descent into Carmel-by-the-Sea. Winding my way through the quaint little tourist town, I find the Green Lantern Inn for my first night's stay. After wheeling my bike into my room, I shower, change into walking-around clothes, and head to town for dinner.

Carmel. Land of the Beautiful People. It's cute and homey. Gives me a warm and comfortable feeling for the start of my adventure. After dinner I walk down to the beach to enjoy a beautiful sunset surrounded by all the Beautiful People. I call my brother Erik and wish him happy birthday. He thinks the trip is dangerous, and has been trying to talk me out of it for months. He's got the worry gene too.

I stand on the beach, talking to Erik, reassuring him that

I'll be fine. He tries one last desperate attempt to convince me to spend the time fishing with him instead, though he and I both know I won't turn back at this point. What Erik probably doesn't feel, though, is just how attractive that safe and comfortable alternative sounds to me right now, as I battle the little claws of doubt that have grown over the past couple of days.

Not that worry is a wholly bad thing. It can certainly help in the decision-making process, so long as it's moderated. In the case of this trip, there are surely things I should worry about—crossing hundreds of miles of desert on a bicycle in the worst month of the year, for example—but should I let that worry keep me from a great adventure? Worry and fear are two sides of the same coin. They can paralyze us if we let them. Or we can turn them to our advantage, and use them as wise counselors, to be ushered from the room once their counsel is heard and understood.

The temptation is to usher fear and worry from the room as soon as possible, before we hear their wise counsel. The emotions that come with fear are uncomfortable. Sitting under a gnarled tree on the beach, bathed in a glorious sunset and a tiny breeze that's salty and cool, I recognize the emotions that come along with fear, and I push them gently aside. Beneath those emotions is an adventure waiting for me, an adventure I've planned for and trained for. An adventure filled with plenty of unknowns, some risks to fear, and buckets full of real life.

I'm bathed in confidence and contentment as I walk back up to the Green Lantern Inn. Not cocky—just content that I sat with my fear, listened to it, absorbed it. Then turned and walked toward the adventure in front of me.

Fear is only as deep as the mind allows.
Japanese proverb

2

"THE ONE" THROUGH BIG SUR

Trees are sanctuaries. Whoever knows how to speak to them, whoever knows how to listen to them, can learn the truth. They do not preach learning and precepts, they preach undeterred by particulars, the ancient law of life.

Hermann Hesse, *Wandering*

DAY 2 · CARMEL TO LUCIA, CALIFORNIA

When planning this trip, I'd expected to ride 110 miles down the coast from Carmel to Cambria this first day out. Prevailing winds from the Northwest are reliable this time of year, so I figured with a big tailwind, why not start off with a bang? But spring rains washed the highway out (as often happens here), so the road was closed at about 60 miles or so south of Carmel.

So I changed my schedule, and the more the change settled in, the more I liked it. It let me dawdle a bit in Carmel, and dawdle a lot in Lucia. Why burn down the coastline all day, when I could sit at Lucia and enjoy the Pacific?

The Green Lantern doesn't serve breakfast until seven, but since this will be a short day, I sleep in and enjoy breakfast. I climb into the saddle and am spinning through the quaint and quiet streets of Carmel by half past seven.

Much too soon, I'm out on the highway and headed south with moderate traffic. The traffic thins with each mile south I progress, making me realize what a stroke of luck the road closure is for me. While it did force me to change my route, and it cut a few miles of coastal riding out of my trip, it's also keeping the motorized tourists away in droves.

Highway 1 (or "the One" to use California speak) down the coast doesn't have much of a shoulder. In fact, in most places, there's no shoulder at all. This isn't a problem for me since the traffic is light, and most of the traffic seems to be locals, and they're accustomed to cyclists and are generally quite courteous.

It's a chilly day, a welcome sun breaking through the clouds only occasionally. A light headwind teases a rolling mist along the highway off and on throughout the day, bathing me in something between fog and very light rain for most of the day. I spend the day in my warmest clothes, including arm and leg warmers.

It's a wonderfully novel morning of riding through a world I never get to experience. Breakers crash against the shore to my right, while steep and lush mountains rise to my left. A deep, wet scent of ocean and forest seeps into me with every breath.

At about twenty miles south of Carmel, the highway dips back into the forest, pulling me through a magical transformation from a breezy open seafront ride to a quiet and still ride through massive redwoods that are hundreds of years old. The road weaves through lush forest studded with redwood giants for about ten miles, a mixture of state park lands and private property with a gentle and hushed quality.

I'm deeper into Big Sur country now, and the sense of remoteness surprises me. Thousands of cars must drive this road each day when it's not closed, enjoying the scenery, buying food and fuel from the little general stores that dot the side of the road occasionally, eating in the quaint little bars and restaurants. Yet, the sense of remoteness remains.

There's a mystique to the place. It feels wild and untamed. Towering redwoods line the road. The unique coastal climate creates a tropical lushness in the forest. My mood and mindset have changed as I've moved into and through the forest. I feel more relaxed, less scattered, more basic. I stop a couple of times next to large redwoods, lean against them, press my hand to the bark. Ancient trees have a wonderful energy. Their time horizon is beyond what we can imagine. Closing my eyes, I can imagine Ents talking in deep and slow voices . . .

I'm reminded of my grandfather and grandmother. He lived to be almost 100, she to 101. Sitting with them always wrapped me in a unique sense of time and significance. The world they were part of was much bigger and broader than mine. I hadn't lived enough years yet to have such a broad world. Yet, while I sat with them, I could *feel* their world. The breadth of it would wrap around me and make me feel a small part of it while we sat together and I listened to their stories.

My world is getting more broad as the years tick past. The things that seemed so urgent and critical to me when my children were young seem less significant now. My perspective has evolved as my world has grown. I can only imagine what it must feel like to view the world with the wisdom earned as a hundred winters pass.

That's why we need extended families. We need grandparents to help raise our children. Their perspective is more broad, and they've hopefully gained wisdom and understanding along the way. While their eyes may have started to dim, they see more clearly than is possible without the experience behind those eyes.

I miss those grandparents, and think of them as I rest my hand on the trunk of an ancient redwood. I imagine them quietly and patiently touching me back through that trunk, smiling, staring from a world too big for me to imagine.

Stopping at a little settlement of sorts, really just a place where there's a restaurant and small grocery, I take in some calories and liquid. The gardens are covered in plants and flowers, folks are relaxed. I'm reminded again of the steady, moderated coastal climate and the remote feel of a little Eden.

The road gently rises and falls through the forest, easy grades winding through a world that's far more vertical than I'm accustomed to, giant redwood bolts reaching into the sky on either side of me. Home for me is the horizontal world of the prairie, with long sweeping lines that reach endlessly across the horizon from one side of the world to the other. The vertical world of this towering forest is magnificent, and just a tiny bit unsettling to me.

At the top of a long, steady climb, the road curves right and opens into a view out across the Pacific, before plunging in a beautiful ribbon through forests and cottages. Leaning back and forth through the curves, I catch snippets of the wide Pacific over my right shoulder, a big smile plastered across my face as I revel in the joyful descent, until the road resolves again to the rhythm of the crashing ocean on my right, mountains steep and lush on my left.

The road climbs and descends, sometimes precariously, curving in and out of the nooks and crannies of the folded mountain coast. Climbing off the bike in Lucia, I look skyward as the rain begins to fall in earnest.

Lucia may have been an actual town in the past, but now all that's there is a lodge and restaurant. It seems to me that I recall John Steinbeck referring to Lucia in his books about the area, so perhaps back in the early part of the last century there was more to the town.

The property seems to have been in the same family's hands for a couple generations. They have a great spot right on the coast and offer lodging and dining in a beautiful setting. A beautiful setting, and the perfect place to run a business. Gliding up to the establishment, I want to see a charming and idyllic little place. However, I'll soon learn that, in many ways, it's a salient example of free enterprise, the declination brought on by nepotism, and the arrogance and sense of entitlement that "ownership" can inspire, all wrapped into a single stop along the highway.

There's not really any awning outside, so I leave my bike leaning against the front of the building, and walk into the tiny general store that is part of the hotel. I have a reservation, and while it's early afternoon, I'm hoping I can get into my room. The cash register at the general store is also the hotel desk, so I ease up to the counter, still dripping with rain.

"Check-in time is four," says the young woman at the front desk. "You'll have to come back then."

"Is there any chance the room will be available before then? I'm on a bicycle and it'd be nice to get inside where it's warm and dry."

"For all I know, the room is ready now, but check-in time is four," she repeats with more than a touch of pretension. "You can leave your bike outside and sit in the restaurant if you're going to eat."

Wow, she must be family. An employee wouldn't keep a job talking to customers like that.

Finding the most protected place I can on the side of the building, I leave my bike outside and walk into the restaurant to have some lunch. The waitress is equally surly, and her good looks lose quite a bit of their luster in the bargain. That's okay, I'm not going to let someone else's bad attitude mess up my beautiful day.

Someplace in the depths of Scandinavia lies the heart of politeness. The closer to that center of politeness you're raised, the more impeccable are your manners. At least my experience has led me to believe this. While I'm eating my mediocre meal, I listen as an elderly couple who sound like they're from Scandinavia walk in and politely ask where they might sit and have coffee. The waitress, who I'm sure must have been raised on the exact opposite side of the universe, lets them know they aren't welcome unless they're going to order a meal.

Really? There's nobody in the place but me. Is she worried

these old folks will take up valuable tip-generating space while they drink their coffee? She certainly just lowered the tip-earning potential of the table I'm sitting at. The elderly couple shuffles back out into the rain, and I wallow in embarrassment for the loutish manners this woman just showed visitors to our country.

Finally, four o'clock rolls around, and I retrieve my key and head for my room. It's a nice view in a romantic and quiet setting, but that's about all that can be said on the "value" side of the equation. The fixtures and decor are several decades old. The plumbing works, mostly. The mold is as I expect in this climate, but the little heater isn't up to the task of keeping the room warm as the night cools down.

My standards for motel rooms are low. Really low. I'm usually happy to stay in a small-town motel that costs $35/night, knowing full-well that it'll be just like this room. Problem is, this room is $200 a night. Really. And the meals are proportionately overpriced. There's a sucker in every crowd, and tonight I'm resigning myself to be that sucker. I need a warm place to stay for the night, and they have a (mostly) warm room for me to rent. I'm able to look at the proprietors in a light that accepts that they're running a business, and they've made choices about how they want to run that business. I don't like it, but I want what they have to sell, and I'm willing to pay for it.

Back at the restaurant for supper, a fellow at a nearby table starts up a conversation. Turns out he's a cyclist too. He lives up in northern California, and is following the same route I am to Paso Robles tomorrow. We share good conversation over supper, swapping stories about the detour we'll need to take tomorrow over the mountains because of the road closure.

We've both been warned repeatedly about how steep and curvy the road is, and while this gives me some concern, I wallow in the unjustified overconfidence of someone who rides and trains in the mountains of Colorado. Tomorrow holds some meaningful lessons in humility for me, though I'm not yet aware of the upcoming class syllabus. For tonight, I'm en-joying my conversation with my new-found comrade, learning quite a bit about minimalist touring on a bicycle from him.

When I started out on this trip, I thought I was carry-ing a pretty small pack of gear. Something between 15 and 20 pounds. I'd included some "nice to have's," but felt justified as I kept the total weight down to under 20 pounds (without water of course). This fella carries a tiny little bag that weighs in at about 7 pounds. Less than half the weight of my gear. I'm fascinated with this approach, but still confident that I'm pack-ing plenty light, and won't have any problems keeping my pace. I simmer in that cocky arrogance while finishing dessert . . .

3

ACROSS THE COASTAL RANGE

Mountains have a way of dealing with overconfidence.
Hermann Buhl

DAY 3 · LUCIA TO PASO ROBLES, CALIFORNIA

Dawn at Lucia is wrapped in a wet mist that brings a hush to the sounds of morning. The folks at the lodge have agreed to set out the breakfast buffet a little early so Dave Meyers and I can get started down the road. (Dave Meyers is the fella I shared supper with last night.) This is a nice gesture that I didn't expect after the contemptuousness I saw yesterday. Dave has gulped down his breakfast and is headed out the door as I'm walking in. We exchange a few pleasantries before he swings into the saddle and pedals down the road in the damp morning air.

With just over 70 miles to go today, I dilly-dally over breakfast. I know there's a steep climb first thing out, but figure it can't be that bad, and then the rest of the day should be easy—especially if that mythical northwest wind comes around today. After breakfast, I walk outside, hanging out and enjoying the beautiful morning.

A car pulls up with two college-aged girls from France. They couldn't afford the prices at the Lucia Lodge, so they'd slept in their car. There are no indoor restrooms at the restaurant, so we're taking turns at the gas-station style restrooms on the outside wall of the Lucia General Store and restaurant. The night was cold, and they look like they didn't get much sleep.

After only a few minutes, we're chatting as-if we're long-time friends, and it strikes me again how readily and quickly fellow travelers pick each other out and bond. It happened yesterday evening with Dave Meyers over dinner. It's happening this morning as I stand in the misty morning air with two young women from France.

Pedaling south along the rugged coastline on a deserted highway, enjoying a beautiful morning light, it occurs to me that I should've offered the girls the use of my room during the morning hours to shower and rest, since it was already paid for. I could have bragged about the two pretty French girls who spent the morning in my hotel room. I would have left out the part about me not being there. Life's about creating good stories . . .

Reaching the detour route, I take a left onto Nacimiento Road, a forest service road that's been paved. Crossing a cattle grate as I leave the highway, I begin a seven mile climb that combines heavenly views with hellacious climbing.

As the climbing begins, I drop into my lowest possible gear, and I'll rarely leave that gear for the next hour and 20 minutes. The climb is about 3000 feet in about seven miles— about 400 feet a mile, an average of 7 to 8 percent. Maybe only 4 to 5 percent in some places, balanced by many places at 11 or 12 percent, a couple places at 16 to 18 percent. The U.S. interstate highway system allows a maximum grade of 6 percent. A 7 to 8 percent grade on a highway is considered dangerous; 9 percent is rarely encountered anywhere.

Pedaling up an 11 or 12 percent grade is gut-wrenching, even without the extra touring weight on the bike. At 16 percent, it's all I can do to keep moving. The climb slaps some of the swagger right out of me, and has me giving serious consideration to those "nice to have" items in my pack. Tomorrow I have a VERY long day of riding, with climbing at the end of the day. Just how "nice" are those extra ounces and pounds I have in my pack?

While pouring my focus into the work of climbing, I also need to keep a little attention aimed at the road ahead and behind. For most of the climb, it would be impossible for two cars to pass each other at speed. The road's just too narrow. When two cars pass, one needs to pull over as far as they can, while the other passes slowly. The constant tight turns and switchbacks limit the opportunity for even that sort of passing.

Notwithstanding the steep grade and narrow road, the beauty of the ride up the west slope of the Coastal Range is hard to express. The views back down onto the coast as I climb are stunning. Time after time, the road makes a sharp switch out on a ledge that gives me a view either north or south along the rugged coastline that takes my breath away. At one point, I'm stopped and admiring the view, eating a banana, when a convertible sports car steams past me headed up the hill. The driver is one of the blonde Beautiful People, sitting so low in the seat she can barely see over the hood. She waves at me as she passes, exclaiming, "Isn't this just so beautiful?!"

Well, yes it is. From the top of this bicycle, with an unlimited view and the time to take it all in safely, it's beautiful indeed.

In those spots where the road tucks back into the mountainside, the landscape changes suddenly to a deeply forested thicket with towering redwoods. The transition from the openness of the mountainside to the depth of the thickets is usually marked by a zone of smaller trees covered in hanging lichens.

The grade gets much easier toward the top, but the temperature has dropped dramatically. I stop several times to enjoy wide vistas with views that seem to go forever back down the mountains and across the Pacific, but the stops are short as the moist air cools me rapidly. At the top of the climb, the road is deep into a forest, the air itself is quite cool, and I'm chilling down even faster. I stop, put on my jacket, and take in some fluid and calories.

Descending is downright cold, and I'm shivering hard. After a few miles of descending through forest, the landscape changes quickly and the temperature climbs. In less than five miles, I'm in a dry, grassy savannah much like my home on the eastern slope of the Rocky Mountains in Colorado.

Nacimiento Road transitions into Fort Hunter-Liggett as the descent flattens out. The traffic is still extremely light, and I can only imagine how light the traffic would be without the road closure back on the coast. A warm tailwind follows me out of the mountains, painting a big smile across on my face.

Winding my way through broad oak savannah, I marvel at the massive old valley oaks spread thinly across the plain. Giant spreading trees, some of them 600 years old, they have massive trunks and beautifully shaped crowns. I stop to enjoy the silence and beauty of the place, leaning my bike against the side of one of these old Ents, and my back against the other side.

This old tree has called this grassy plain home for hundreds of years. Basking in the bright sun, soaking up nutrients from the ground, it's grown to this nobility at a pace I can't comprehend. It welcomes me under its shade, and I wonder what other folks looked like and sounded like who might have shared this shade in the past, over the hundreds of years that this old graybeard has been growing in this spot, quietly waiting for me.

I'm in Steinbeck country now, broad grassy pastures with scattered ancient trees. I imagine Samuel Hamilton jostling down the road toward me in a wagon, Lee sitting beside me in the shade. A small breeze whispers through the grass close to me as I lay against the old oak tree, a touch of sun making its way through the branches now and then to warm me, the sea of short prairie grass stretching out for several hundred yards between this tree and the next. Relaxation saturates my body as my mind brims with contentment. Soft savannah sounds fade into the distance as I doze up to the edge of a nap.

Paso Robles, CA

Victorville, CA

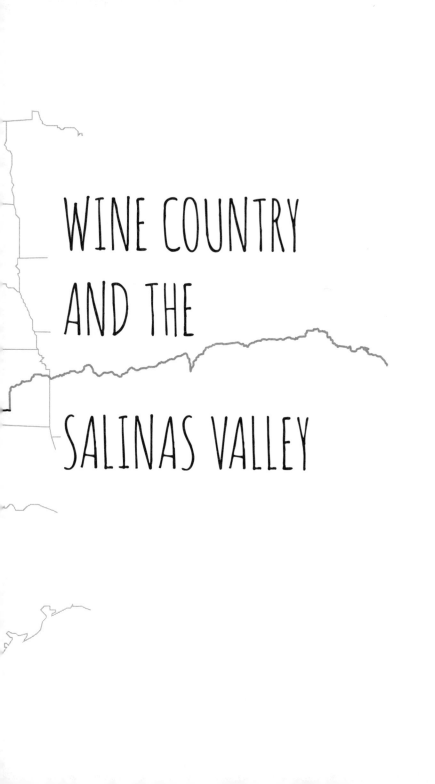

WINE COUNTRY AND THE

SALINAS VALLEY

4

BUGS AND MINIMALISM

There is more refreshment and stimulation in a nap,
even of the briefest, than in all the alcohol ever distilled.
Ovid

PASO ROBLES, CALIFORNIA

My mind drifting lazily along the edge of sleep, my body free-falling into deep rest following the punishing climb I put it through earlier, I pull my consciousness back into the quiet and peaceful meadow around me, and keep moving down the road. The wind shifts, and I face a growing breeze as I travel in a more southerly direction. I stop at a tiny general store at a crossroads called Lockwood, and eavesdrop on a conversation some locals are having. A gal has gotten a new job with the county, and she's telling her friends all about it. After her friends leave, I go over and talk to her.

Turns out she catches bugs. I'm in wine country now, and folks here go to great lengths to assure that certain particularly destructive bugs don't get a foothold in their region. She goes around all day setting traps, and investigating what she catches.

She's really excited about her job and what she does, and tells me *way* more than I need or want to know about bugs. But I enjoy the lesson and the chat, then saddle up and make my way down the road, leaving her making notes about bugs in her bug book.

Another 20 miles down the road is a little intersection called Bee Rock, where I catch up with Dave Meyers and we enjoy a sandwich together. Like Lockwood, there's nothing here but a store. It's a friendly place, with tables out on the deck. Dave and I enjoy a nice long lunch out on the deck, chatting and enjoying the beautiful day. I'm ready to leave a little before Dave is, so I bid goodbye and start turning the pedals again, headed up the road toward Paso Robles.

Paso Robles is smaller than I expected. It's probably not much more than a mile from the north end of town to the south. It's a quaint little town, and very bicycle friendly. I get a cozy homecoming sensation when I see my hotel, anticipating a warm shower and soft bed.

The young fellow behind the desk checking me in has a name tag that says "James," and it turns he's a cyclist. "Where'd ya ride from?" James asks.

I tell him my route from today, and he smiles and nods. "I've done that ride several times, over and back in a day. It's a great ride, isn't it?"

Over and back in a day? That's 150 miles, with steep climbing. This guy's an animal. I'm tuckered out after doing just half the ride. I try to keep the wimp factor as low as possible when I reply. "Absolutely, a beautiful ride. I'll bet it's a sweet day going over and back in a day."

"Yeah, we usually ride over in the morning, have lunch at Lucia, then ride back after lunch. Steep coming up the Nacimiento Road, eh?"

My eyebrows climb my forehead. "Steep doesn't start to describe it! I thought I was gonna fall over a couple times."

His laugh is full of enjoyable nostalgia, his eyes looking off into the distance, as memories of what were probably wonderful rides wash over his face. Looking back at me, he asks, "So, where ya riding tomorrow?"

"Tomorrow's a really big day for me—I need to end up in Frazier Park."

I watch the joy of pleasant memories drain from his face, replaced by the agony of remembered pain. "I did that ride once. Hardest day I ever spent on a bicycle. Hell spread out over 150 miles. The winds across the valley spend the day sucking the soul out of you. Then the climb at the end of the day drops the hammer of ultimate despair on any joy left in whatever shell remains."

Uh, oh. I might have bitten off just a bit more than I can chew. James must have seen the look on my face, and tries to give me some encouragement. "But hey, maybe the winds won't be bad for you, ya know? But either way, be sure and carry lots of water, because it's a long way across that valley from here until you can fill your water bottles—something like 75 miles, right?"

I'm not really feeling any better. "Right. Thanks. Yeah, 75 miles."

Falling back into his front desk persona, he continues, "You're in room 327, Mr. Hanson. Be sure and let us know if we can get anything for you, and I hope you enjoy your stay with us. Oh, and good luck on your ride tomorrow!"

"Thanks, I appreciate that. Oh, one other thing. James, is there a way I can package up a few things and have you ship them for me?"

After a hot shower, I spread my stuff out on the bed. Sorting through it with more ruthlessness than I had back at home before I started the ride, I build a pile of "nice to have" items, ready to package up and ship back to Colorado. In the pile is my iPad, iPod, tiny speaker, Kindle, 700-lumen headlight, all the chargers associated with this electronic stuff, 4 of my tire tubes (leaving me still with 4), and a few other items. While I don't put stuff on the scale, it seems to me that I've cut my weight in half.

When I packed for the trip, I wanted to stay under 20 pounds. I was able to do this while still including quite a few items that I might find handy. The iPad is only a couple pounds, the Kindle maybe a pound, the light a couple pounds. It all fit inside my 20 pound goal—why not take it?

My culture teaches that it's *good* to have everything you might need. Having something is good, being without something is bad. When I was packing, my perspective was, "how much can I take, within my constraints?" Tonight, looking down at the gear spread out on the bed, I was asking myself, "how little do I need to survive?"

Minimalism. Simplicity.

Stuff adds up if you're not careful. It builds up around you. Getting rid of stuff brings a cleansing sensation. Almost like "stuff" weighs down the soul. It happens to me when I clean stuff out of my house too: a liberating sense, a lightness, after I go through and give away or toss large swaths of stuff.

When I was younger, I was more focused on accumulating than on distributing and cleansing. Now, I find myself constantly reevaluating just how much stuff I want around me. How much clutter can I tolerate before it weighs on my soul? How much flotsam am I willing to wade through to see the world around me clearly? It keeps me from moving along the path. Each "thing" I accumulate attaches a string deep into my heart and soul, connecting me to the thing itself, making continued movement down the path difficult. An addiction to accumulation maybe? A cultural epidemic?

My extra flotsam on this bike ride is one tiny symptom, but it's all around us. Look at how much of our life's energy we put into "accumulating wealth." We advertise how much wealth we've accumulated with the homes we live in, the cars we drive, and our pride in our continued pursuit of greater wealth.

But all our wealth weighs us down. It's too much to try and haul up the steep hills of the back roads of life. Instead, we stay on the flat and busy expanse of the masses, where we don't need to confront the tough climbs that might be encountered in the wilderness of discovering ourselves.

The sweetest moments in life lay waiting along the steep and winding backroads. They're often hidden among difficult questions and tough issues. Sorting through and finding them sometimes requires deep and honest introspection. But these steep and meandering backroads might be one of the best places in life to find glimpses of heaven, and to discover what that means to each of us.

Wasn't this a common message among the great sages of the last few thousand years? Jesus was pretty clear when admonishing followers to avoid the temptations of accumulating wealth. Easier for a camel to pass through the eye of a needle, he said, than for a wealthy man to find heaven.

That's on my mind this evening, as I look with satisfaction at the pile of "stuff" I'm sending back home. The last thing I want is seven or eight extra pounds in my bag that might slow me down if I catch a little glimpse of heaven somewhere along the road.

5

HATE RADIO AND SWALLOWED PRIDE

"There is, I believe, in every disposition a tendency to some particular evil, a natural defect, which not even the best education can overcome."

"And your defect is a propensity to hate everybody."

"And yours," he replied with a smile, "is willfully to misunderstand them."

Jane Austen, *Pride and Prejudice*

DAY 4 · PASO ROBLES TO LEBEC, CALIFORNIA

The tiny sliver of early dawn creeps into the eastern sky as I fill my water bottles and gather calories at the convenience store on my way out of Paso Robles. It's cold this morning—35 degrees. The ride through town and out into the countryside east of town is quiet as the cold air draws a constant shiver from me.

The first faint light in the eastern sky reveals wide and rolling wine country around me, vineyards lying like quilts across the twilight landscape that rolls endlessly toward the horizon. It's dead calm in the pre-dawn chill, the crisp air becoming a little more tolerable as I put more coal to the pedals, maintaining a healthy pace to generate heat.

As the sun crests the horizon, I hear the pounding of hooves on my left. I hadn't noticed the horse track over there in the low light, punctuated by beautiful buildings that whisper words like *genteel* with a cultivated accent. A couple of folks are out running horses on the track at this early hour, and I stop for a minute to admire the beauty of the scene with the brightening eastern horizon behind them, but the chilly air quickly pushes me back into the saddle to pedal.

The passing miles bring a small change in the landscape around me, the rolling hills evolving into something more like a remote steppe. I'm following Highway 58 across an open and arid region that reminds me a lot of eastern Colorado and Western Kansas. The traffic is extremely light, with a car passing me every 10 minutes or so. A headwind is growing, and with it grows my worry.

With 146 miles planned for the day, a headwind is something I can't afford. Even with no wind at all, it'll be a tough day for me, and I'll be lucky to finish by dark. My only chance of making this a manageable day is the fabled northwest wind that I've yet to experience on this ride.

I gear down as the headwind grows, slowing my pace further. Options and likely scenarios play through my mind, and I consider ways to avoid riding into the middle of the night. At 75 miles, I'll connect with Highway 33, and have several miles of extremely dangerous highway to ride, with no shoulder and very heavy truck traffic. With just a few miles to go before this intersection, I stop along the side of the road to eat a granola bar, and conclude that the best and safest course for the day will be to try and hitch a ride past the dangerous section of highway.

Leaning against my bike along the side of the road, crunching my granola bar, I realize how unlikely it is that somebody will pick up a hitchhiker out here in the middle of nowhere. The wind blows some dust across the road, and way back down the road, I see a vehicle approaching. I continue to crunch on my granola bar, recognizing the vehicle as a pickup truck when it's only a quarter mile away. "What the heck," I think to myself when the truck is only a few hundred yards away, and stick my thumb out.

The turning wheel of karma smiles down on me. I stand dumbstruck as the shiny new pickup pulls up alongside me. The driver agrees to haul me past the upcoming nasty section of road, laughing at the idea of riding a bike on that section, emphasizing that he barely feels safe driving his truck on it.

From the radio in the truck a hate-spewing radical preaches at us, ladling propaganda into our brains. The driver has clearly consumed his allotted portions of propaganda in the past, because he knows all about who the bad guys are, and who can be blamed for which crisis we face. Of course, a crisis doesn't need to be actual or factual to be useful, so long as it helps the listener to maintain the proper level of hate toward the designated bad guys.

The ride gives me time to down a bottle of water and a little food while enjoying the absurdity of the radio blather, wondering just how long we can last as a nation when there are so many folks like this out there. When I saw the movie *Idiocracy*, I thought it was funny. Each passing year seems to bring us closer to that reality. It's less funny now, and more disturbing.

Grateful for the ride, I figure listening to this fella rant about the world he wants to believe exists is just payment for the ride. Although some part of me would like to ride further in this nice air-conditioned truck, I realize I need to get back to the real world. As I'm climbing out of the cab, he comments that he's getting low on gas. I drop him a twenty, and thank him for the ride.

Climbing back on my bike, turning the pedals once again, I shake the nonsense out of my tiny little brain. I've always been a pretty strong believer in the constitutional right to vote, and the need for everyone to exercise that right. But as I think about it, some sort of basic test of a person's ability to discern fact from fiction, truth from propaganda, might not be a bad idea.

6

BROKEN ROADS AND DESERT DOGS

*Inside of me there are two dogs. One of the dogs is
mean and evil. The other dog is good. The mean dog
fights the good dog all the time. Which dog wins?
The one I feed the most.*

Comanche elder speaking of the inner struggle of good and evil

DAY 5 · LEBEC TO VICTORVILLE, CALIFORNIA

All eyes turn toward me as I walk into the breakfast room at
the trucker's motel in Lebec. My spandex shorts and bright
yellow windbreaker standing out like a ballerina in a rodeo
arena. Ignoring the stares, I grab a plateful of calories and plop
myself down in a seat. The good buddies in the room decide
I'm not that interesting after all.

I smile as I think about the scene from *Star Wars*:

"These aren't the droids we're looking for."

"Move along."

When Obi-wan did it in the movie, it seemed like magic.
But I think it's just part of being human. If you accept a certain
viewpoint or perspective as good, right and factual, and exude
this into the space around you with confidence, then the folks

around you seem to *catch* what you're exuding. Sounds kind of New-Age-y, but it really seems to be how we work.

I think back to the fella who gave me a lift past the bad section of road yesterday. He absolutely accepted as fact the complete fiction that his media masters had been pouring into his brain every day. If they say it's fair and balanced, then it must be, right? If they say I should be outraged, then I should be.

A room full of truckers in flannel shirts and dirty ball caps look at this odd duck walk into the room. He's wearing a do-rag on his head, spandex shorts, and a bright windbreaker. He's greatly outnumbered, perfect fodder for some early-morning harassing. Instead, the truckers all shrug their shoulders and go on about their business, accepting me without comment. All because I believe I belong there.

Be the Force . . .

My imagined Jedi powers have no ability to warm me in the pre-dawn chill. I find myself dilly-dallying in the warmth of the convenience store. I know I've got a descent first thing this morning, and I'm not looking forward to the icy wind.

It's 35 degrees outside and a bitter wind blows through the pass. With full water bottles and pockets full of food, I'm grateful for the little bit of work that a half mile of climbing offers to reach the high-point of the pass. Warmed just a little, a blast of cold wind coming over the pass slaps me in the face, and I start an ice-cold descent.

I'm shivering hard as I pass through the little town of Gorman, which is one of the oldest continuously used roadside rest stops in California, dating to way before the time of cars and highways. This route was heavily used by Native American Tataviam people for centuries before the Spanish entered the area. Apparently the town is built on the site of the Tataviam village of Kulshra'jek.

I'm fascinated by roads and their history. Roads are the arteries that weave a civilization together. The settlements that spring up, evolve, and fade along those arteries are, in many ways, the definition of the civilization. As the traffic along a trading path grows, it becomes wider, and pretty soon it's called a road. Technology enables machines that travel the roads, so the roads have to be improved and paved. Pretty soon, you've got a web of roads and highways used by millions, and a few of those are evolutions of a little dirt path once used by traders in the area.

Our lives are like that. Who we are is defined by the paths we've chosen in life. Some of those paths get reinvented and improved as we travel them; while others fall into disrepair as we abandon them. It's nice to occasionally find the time to look back across a path well-traveled, see the changes our path has wrought in us, and the changes we've left behind us along the path.

There are some things in life that bring a deep "joy smile" to our faces. A baby's smile when he sees his mother's face. A lover who sees her beau after a long absence. Maybe an elephant standing at the edge of a cool lake on a hot day, spraying water on himself and feeling the refreshing coolness. A dog who's found something particularly aromatic to roll around in, coming to his feet, shaking off and smiling at his new perfume.

For a cyclist, a gentle downhill grade with a tailwind creates that smile. Once I'm past the bitter cold and aching fingers of the first half hour of the day, that smile splits my face from ear to ear as I soak up a wonderful tailwind flying down a gentle grade toward Palmdale.

After a few miles I come to an accident in the clean-up process. There's a line of cars waiting to get by, but it looks like they're going to be there a while. I glide up to the front along the shoulder, and the patrolman waves me through. Now, life is getting downright magnificent! Until he opens that lane up, I've got zero traffic coming behind me. I grab the biggest gear I can find, and fly down the road as hard as I can.

The scenery around me transforms rapidly from the moderately wooded mountain pass around Frazier Park into the edge of a world with very little water. By the time I cross Highway 14 and make my way into Lancaster, there's no doubt I've arrived in the desert.

Rolling into the town of Lancaster at 9:00 a.m., I've already covered 50 miles for the day. I find a little Mexican cantina and eat a breakfast of fish and beans. Judging from the bars on the windows, and the run-down condition of most of the buildings, this is not a great part of town. One of the downsides of cycling on backroads is that you sometimes end up in places you wouldn't have ended up in otherwise. Of course, that's also one of the upsides—you end up in places you wouldn't have otherwise . . .

Talking with the hombre who runs the cantina is both entertaining and challenging for both of us. His English isn't very good, and my Spanish is worse, but somehow we communicate well enough for him to give me good advice on making my way through town toward Victorville. It turns out that the Palmdale/Lancaster area is a giant sprawl, 20 or 30 miles across. I suspect many of the people who live here commute into LA. It has the feel of a big city, even though there's no real "city."

Picking my way east through Palmdale and Lancaster, the condition of the pavement has evolved past inconvenient, well into hazardous. Giant fissures weave their way from edge to edge across the pavement, a mosaic of danger for the cyclist.

The "taxpayer revolts" of the eighties in California have come home to roost here as the state often lives on the precipice of bankruptcy. One of the glaring symptoms of the devastated financial condition they've created for themselves is the condition of their secondary roads and highways.

This all ties back to that "evolution of roads" thing, both literally and figuratively. I hear people talk about the financial condition of California, blaming current decisions and current politicians. Reality is that current financial conditions are rarely a result of recent decisions. California put itself on this path 30 years ago. Want to know how you got to where you are today? Don't look at the last mile of the road you're on, look at choices you made way back down the road; those are the choices that put you where you are today.

This is true in every aspect of life. Whether it's national politics, the national economy, the state of my personal net worth, the condition of the truck I drive, or the state of the relationships in my life. Unless we see this, and understand our decisions clearly, we can't possibly hope to find a way out of the desert we've put ourselves in. The road is rocky and broken now, and getting back onto clean pavement requires that we understand those wrong turns we've been taking for quite a ways back down the road.

My wheels are rolling across a broken road this morning. I think it'd be hard to find a ten square foot section of this pavement that isn't fissured with cracks large enough to swallow a bicycle tire, so riding takes more concentration to stay upright than it would on decent pavement.

I'm well past Lancaster and Palmdale, concentrating on keeping my tires out of fissures in the road, when angry barking catches my attention. I haven't noticed the high-fenced yard around a dilapidated house coming up on my left. The angry barking coming from the dogs on the other side of that fence has my full attention now. These are clearly mean and nasty dogs. They know they're mean and nasty, and they want everyone around to know they're mean and nasty.

Approaching their territory, I'm comforted by the high chain link fence running along the road, keeping the dogs in. The dogs are pouring toward the fence as I pass the front of the house, and I notice they're headed toward the gate, where there's a big gap in the fence.

It's rare that I worry much about dogs. I get along great with them for the most part, and it's usually clear they're just letting me know I'm passing their territory. But right now, there's no doubt in my mind these dogs mean business. They have no interest in scaring me off; they want warm flesh.

There are six or eight of these guys, snapping at each other for the honor of drawing first blood. Before I've even thought about it, I'm out of the saddle, and the adrenaline has cranked my output up into the red zone. I'm pouring as much coal as I can to the pedals, and the 35 miles per hour I'm able to reach keeps me just ahead of the fastest of the dogs.

After a few seconds of slow-motion terror, I see I'm leaving them behind, so I start to back off the speed. Normally, once a dog chases you out of his territory, he's fine if you slow down. He's done his duty, and moved you along the road. He's not in this for blood; he just wants to keep the peace in his territory. He's the sheriff, and he's moved the vagrant out of town.

I don't think these guys are wearing badges. They're the desperadoes, and they *are* in it for blood. I'm 50 yards ahead of them, and they had backed off when they realized they couldn't catch me. But when they see me slowing down, their interest in the chase renews with vigor. Immediately they begin sprinting up the road toward me again, hopeful that their prey might be faltering, fighting to be the one to bring me down. Of course, I crank the effort up again—this time leaving them far behind before slowing. I'm several miles up the road before I stop checking over my shoulder from time to time.

The wind continues to shift as the day moves along. This morning's friendly wind has turned decidedly hostile, the hostility growing rapidly. By the time I'm approaching Adelanto, the gale in my face has slowed my progress to under 10 miles per hour. The profanity pouring out of my mouth increases incrementally with the wind's ferocity.

My labored pedaling is moving me slowly south along Bellflower Street, completely beat and broken by the merciless tempest in my face. Up ahead I spot a low little brick wall on my right. I need a rest. Just a little respite from the remorseless punishment I'm feeling.

Sitting down on the grass behind the little brick wall, my body and soul sigh with a tiny little relief, as the howl of air racing past my ears abates. Sipping water, chewing on a granola bar, I look over to my left, and see a lady sitting in a car twenty feet away or so. She's the crossing guard, waiting for the kids to get out of school, and I hope she hasn't called the cops about this weird guy skulking around the school yard. She smiles at me though, and I smile back. She will have to stand out in that wind to help the kids across the street, and understands exactly why I'm hiding behind the wall.

Again, I pass through a moment of connection with someone along the road. We don't speak, and never see each other except through her windshield. But we share the wind as our common enemy today.

May the Force be with you.

It's close to 5:00 when I finally arrive at my hotel in Victorville. My last three miles are a terrifying negotiation along a packed frontage road beside I-15. The wind punishes me as impatient drivers crowd me to the edge of the road. While there have been aspects of today that have been truly sweet, I'm happy to be done with vicious dogs, brutal headwinds, and appalling roads.

After a warm shower and good dinner, I'm amazed at just how good I feel. I have every reason to feel beat-down and dejected right now, but I don't. I'm hopeful for a good wind and improved roads tomorrow. I remember with fondness the first 50 miles of the day, letting the last 70 fade away. I've only got 80 miles to ride tomorrow, and I'm already anticipating the rest day following those 80 miles.

The human mind can do pretty cool things with hope. Hope and anticipation of my upcoming rest day has washed the dirt and grime of mean dogs, bad roads, and nasty winds right off my emotional canvas.

I live a privileged life, with few hardships. What keeps folks going who're born in the wrong place at the wrong time, living in utter misery, surviving some of the horrible tragedy and hardship that life can dish out? Hope, it seems, is the bridge that spans the gap between the unbearable today and the dreamed tomorrow. So long as we have that bridge of hope to stand on, the misery of the past drifts off into the fog behind us. Looking back, we tend not to see what's shrouded in the fog, and instead see the peaks and high points we've come through.

I'm learning to appreciate the beauty of the simplicity I'm finding on this ride. I get on my bike in the morning, and I ride. I find food and drink, and I ride. I'm alone with my thoughts in the saddle all day long . . . and I find I like the company I'm keeping.

DESERTS

1

THE SILENCE OF WIND AND SAND

Silence is the language of God, all else is poor translation.
Rumi

DAY 6 · VICTORVILLE TO TWENTYNINE PALMS, CALIFORNIA

The earliest hint of light finds me wheeling my bike out of the hotel in Victorville. Following Highway 18 east into the little town of Lucerne Valley, I stop at what will likely be my last available water supply for 50 miles. Here, I leave Highway 18, and head further east on Old Woman Springs Road. (It's also called Highway 247, but that's a boring name . . .)

With no shoulder on the highway, I'm thankful for the very light traffic early on this beautiful Saturday morning. A fickle wind swirls in the mounting heat of the morning.

The wildlife along the road has changed with the land-scape as I've moved further into the desert. For several miles, I pay close attention to chirping along the side of the road, as-suming it must be some sort of ground bird. Eventually, I come to the conclusion that the chirping comes from small lizards (or maybe geckos) dashing across the road from one scrap of vegetation to another. I suspect they hole up in the shade as the day heats up, but here in the early morning, I can barely see them as the scurry across the pavement.

I also notice something less. Less noise. It's really quiet. A mesmerizing quiet.

I pull over to have a little snack in the deepening quiet. A fierce and piercing sun scorches the desert floor around me, pushing the temperature upwards. I can see for tens of miles all around me, and it feels like the quiet reaches out across all those miles of baking desert. The light and silent wind swirls around here and there, playing across my skin, swirling dust in the road, hinting of a big wind to come.

Out here in the wide-open desert, with the barest of vegetation spread sparsely across the wind-swept sand, there's no instrument for the wind to play, no grass to whisper through, no leaves to rustle.

I lean against my bike in the stillness for a long time, appreciating the silence. It's a rare sense of quiet so deep it's almost fragrant, and I find myself tasting the air for the scent of this wonderful thing around me. Savoring the tranquility, I'm reminded of a scuba diving experience from years ago.

It was a night dive. Moving along the top of a reef, enjoying the nighttime creatures, I noticed the occasional hunting shark, a large octopus now and then searching for prey. Coming to an open sandy area, I settled down to suspend just above the bottom, and turned out my light. The darkness enveloped me completely. The silence was breathtaking. I lay there for a few minutes, slowing my breath and heart rate, enjoying the silent primordial darkness. I was alone in an environment that could rapidly turn mortally hostile, and I temporarily shut down my important sense, my sense of sight. I surrendered to the environment around me, allowing myself to soak inside the vastness, the only sound that of the bubbles from my relaxed breath through the regulator.

The memory of that silent reef returns to me out here on the bright, silent surface of the desert. What attracts me to these moments out on the edge of comfort? What is it that wandering alone with the quiet unlocks within me? Basking in the solitude. Feeling a glimpse of something greater than myself.

Climbing back in the saddle, I pedal down the road, feeling the growing wind in my face. I gear down and notch my speed back. How quickly a smile can flip into a frown with the shifting of the wind.

With each passing mile, the traffic increases. A narrow highway with no shoulder, I'm feeling pressed to the side of the road by drivers clearly angry that I'm riding on *their* road. My frown over the wind now mixes with real fear of the impatient drivers flying past me with inches to spare at 70 miles per hour.

8

MUSTANG TERROR

For what is it to die,
But to stand in the sun and melt into the wind?
Kahlil Gibran

MORTALITY VISITED

Pressing up a gentle slope into the headwind, I hear the roar of
a car engine ahead. Coming toward me a Mustang pulls out to
pass another car. Expletives explode from my mouth as I make
a split-second decision to stay on the road rather than diving
off the shoulder and down the two foot drop into the rocks
below. Pulling out right behind the Mustang is a pickup truck.

Rocketing head-on at highway passing speed, they pass
me at a couple feet, though it feels like inches. I've got no
shoulder. Nowhere to retreat. I'm completely exposed and
vulnerable, left to trust completely, trusting both the drivers
and the wheel of karma.

The terror of the moment grips me as I continue pedaling, and I begin shaking. Luck is with me this morning, but
just barely. So easily, that close encounter could have gone
the other way.

There are moments in life that come down to a tiny fraction of fate or fortune, and can go either way. There's a new lens that opens up to us suddenly when this happens, and we see the world a little differently. We realize that we just stumbled past the doorstep that takes us out of this life. Stealing a glance into the doorway as we pass, death's merciless scythe reaches out to leave a little scar on our soul, reminding us just how closely the door follows us through life.

What we see when we glance in as we pass does much to define our spiritual outlook. We look back on these moments, basking in the mercy and grace we feel at being still on this side of the doorway. From these moments we decide whether we believe there's any rhyme or reason to which way we stumbled. We wonder if we're somehow favored by the Universe, or somehow invincible, or deserving of some special treatment.

The jitters and shakes eventually subside with my regular pedal strokes. I realize how dang lucky I am to be alive. With passing weeks and months I'll look back on the panic and dread of the moment, and I'll remember that dark door through which I stole a glance in passing. I'll remember the sense of overwhelming grace and mercy I felt when my stumble kept me on this side of that door. I'll realize, over and over, that at any moment "there but for Grace" I could easily fall.

There's no deserving, or plan, or roadmap, or anything like that. There's no bartering or negotiating. Lean just slightly the wrong way, at the wrong time, and the door will swallow us up if we happen to pass too close.

Reach out and hold hands with Grace, give Mercy a hug. Today and every day of this lifetime. That's the image that will come back to me over time as I remember that stolen glance into darkness. Not because of any debt. Not to buy insurance for the next stumble.

Just because. Those moments introduce us to Grace and Mercy. The gift is the chance to reach out and hold their hands. Nothing more, nothing less.

9

THE CAROUSEL

Every time I see an adult on a bicycle, I no longer despair for the future of the human race.

H. G. Wells

INTO TWENTYNINE PALMS

Reaching Highway 62 and turning east, the southwest wind that was in my face before now becomes a tailwind. A gentle elevation drop for the final 15 miles, and a great shoulder on the road, make for a delightful salve with which to drown the near terror of those final miles on Old Woman Springs Road.

Rolling up to the stoplight in the town of Joshua Tree, a long line of motorcycles approaches from behind me. The leading motorcycles pull up beside me as I wait for the light to change. They're chatting back and forth, trying to decide if this is where they should turn right to get to Joshua Tree National Park.

They look at me, "We turn right here to get to the park, right?"

I nod and point my thumb to the right. They pass the word back behind them that this is where they turn.

"Hey, thanks man," a couple of them say as they all swarm around the corner and down the road into the park. The deep rumble of their motors vibrates through me as they flow around and past me. I'm glad the most noise my bike makes is a quiet little chain noise now and then when it needs oil.

Pedaling down the highway again, I recognize a camaraderie I feel with these bikers. These guys are usually decked out to look as tough as they can, with leather and tattoos and loud bikes; a decided contrast to my spandex and a shiny white bicycle. (Hey, at least I have a leather saddle . . .) Occasionally I'll run across bikers who are clearly scornful of cyclists, especially in cities. But out on the open road, it's far more common to have bikers give me the "biker wave" as they pass, and give me plenty of room when they go around me. I often strike up conversations with bikers at diners and gas stations, and there's usually a strong sense that we share the unspoken camaraderie of two wheels on the open road.

I think those of us on two wheels feel a bit disconnected from the enclosed vehicles that represent the safe, status quo in the world. I like the image of a *frontiersman* riding out in the open on two wheels, akin to the horseman who's part of the world he rides through, rather than a spectator who experiences the world filtered through steel and glass. On two wheels, we feel the heat of the sun on our backs, we breathe in the nuance of the scent around us. We're *experiencing* the world of the road, not watching it from a climate controlled rolling theatre. We feel the wind buffeting our face or pushing us gently from behind.

Approaching Twentynine Palms, I stop at a funky little used book store on the side of the road. After 30 minutes of browsing through the jammed isles, I finally settle on a book by an author I've never heard of; the story is about a Ute family in southern Colorado at the turn of the last century. Tomorrow is a rest day, and a book to read will be nice.

Arriving in Twentynine Palms, I stop at the Carousel Cafe. This is exactly the kind of place I love to eat, a local diner where

I'm the only stranger who's walked through the door all day and the waitress greets most folks by name.

My waitress is a gal who's clearly spent most of her life falling into the *attractive* category, but is not accepting age gracefully. She's flirty and saucy, but I'm too worn-out to return her flirtations. All I really care about is the chili dog and hamburger I've ordered.

At least that's my perspective. Her version might read somewhat differently:

> *A middle-aged guy riding a bicycle came in*
> *and ate like a teenage boy. He probably spent*
> *most of his life in the* good shape *category, but*
> *isn't accepting age gracefully. He must have no*
> *common sense, riding his bicycle across the desert*
> *in the summer at his age. A stupid thing to do at*
> *any age, riding across the desert at his age in the*
> *summer is just crazy. He'll probably be roadkill*
> *in another day or two. I was nice to him though,*
> *poor old guy.*

10

THE SEVENTH DAY, RESTING

Don't underestimate the value of Doing Nothing,
of just going along, listening to all the things you
can't hear, and not bothering.
Pooh's Little Instruction Book, inspired by A. A. Milne

DAY 7 · TWENTYNINE PALMS

Day 7 of my trip. A good day to rest. This seems to be a some-what popular opinion at any rate.

Early morning, my favorite time of day. There aren't many folks up and about early, so it always feels like I've got the cosmos to myself. Well, maybe not the cosmos, but this morning I have the hotel lobby and breakfast area to myself. I read the paper while the breakfast counter is set up, then enjoy a quiet and peaceful breakfast outside in the cool shade by the pool.

After a couple hours, some youngsters start to stake their claim to the pool, and I head back in to the breakfast area to enjoy a little second breakfast. There are quite a few folks in here now, and listening to the chatter around me, I'm able to deduce that both a wedding party and a small group of young men from the nearby Marine Corps training center stayed at the hotel last night. There's every indication that some of the young Marines got to know some of the wedding party as the orbits of their respective parties overlapped during a progressively unbridled evening.

Isn't love grand? Well, maybe not love, but at least everyone seems to feel better this morning. Well, okay, maybe not better in all respects. There are clearly some hangovers being carefully nursed. Well, okay, in the case of the Marines, their leader seems none too tender with them in his "nursing" of their hangovers.

But something's certainly grand, you can feel it as the two parties rub shoulders this morning. Though I didn't appreciate the extra noise created by their exuberance last night, I'm certainly appreciating the interesting energy in the breakfast area this morning. Young men pursuing pretty girls. Young girls returning the flirtation just enough to keep the interest going. Young men not sure what to do next, trying to decide if their flirtation is being returned, analyzing, looking for words and facts. Young women stepping in to rescue the situation . . .

I walk out into the shade of the canopy at the front of the building, to check and see which way the wind is blowing. A soft desert breeze from the west caresses my cheek, building my hope for that same wind to blow against my back tomorrow. With hope in my heart, and the recently observed young love from the dining room still in my mind, every breath I take feels like I'm drinking in goodness.

Chatting with a fellow who's smoking a cigarette, he comments that it must be nice to have a day to "do nothing." I think about his comment. Am I really doing nothing?

I plan to enjoy a walk to town to poke around a bit, maybe stop at the grocery and pick up supplies for tomorrow. I plan to enjoy every step I take along that walk. I expect a nap will call to me early in the afternoon, inviting me to wallow in that sweet place just on the margin of sleep for 15 or 20 minutes. I suspect I'll sit in the shade beside the pool later in the afternoon, listening to kids play and parents gossip, enjoying the book I picked up yesterday in the musty bookstore. The promise of this rest day has been up in the forefront of my mind during some tough moments over the past several days, and I plan to sip every possible molecule of enjoyment from it. Doing nothing? Hardly.

Late in the morning, sitting in some shade close to the pool, I'm enjoying my little slice of life. I've got my book with me, but I'm not reading it. I'm languishing in the shade, soaking in the hot air. Kids laughing and splashing in the water around me is a sweet melody, bringing back memories of when my children were young.

I notice a small bird moving around the desert plants, and reflect on how the wildlife has changed along with the plant life as I've moved from the coast out to the desert. In just a few short days I've gone from lush rainforest, through wine country and grassy savannah, now onto a high desert, about to drop into deep and dangerous desert.

One thing I didn't count on when I planned this trip was how full of blooms the desert is in June. The spectacular Datura grows everywhere along the highway here, with beautiful big white flowers that look iridescent in the bright morning sunlight. As the day heats up, the flowers must close or fade, because I don't see them in the afternoon heat. (Of course, they might be there and I'm the one wilted in the afternoon heat, no longer paying close attention . . .) Their large leaves and flowers spread out over the side of the road, spilling their sweet fragrance through the morning air as I've pedaled past them on the road.

Leaning back in my chair, enjoying the shade by the pool, that sweet fragrance infuses my memory. I can surely recall a few frustrating incidents I've had as I've approached this rest day, some bad wind and deadly drivers for example. But along with those moments of frustration has come a long list of moments of pure sweetness.

There's some measure of sweetness in nearly every moment, along with some measure of bitterness. Life is so much better when we learn how to sniff out the sweetness in each moment, distilling any bitterness away.

My eyes close as I wander through these thoughts. The kids have gone in, leaving behind a pristine quiet to keep me company as I sit alone in the warm shade. Drifting along the quiet surface of deep relaxation, sneaking gently along the shore between sleep and wakefulness, I feel a smile in my soul. My mind quietly laps up against that sweet shore of sleep, like a log might roll gently back and forth against a shady bank at the edge of a quiet pond.

11

THE MOJAVE

The quieter you become the more you are able to hear.

Rumi

Day eight, 3:59 a.m. I'm lying awake in bed, looking at the clock, waiting for the wake-up call.

I'm not sure why I ever ask for a wake-up call or set an alarm. It's only if I want to make sure I wake before 4:30 or 5:00 that I use any sort of alarm. When I do, invariably, I'll wake a minute or two before the alarm, and wait for it to go off.

This inner alarm clock started when I was about 11 years old. We were spending a week in a cabin on a lake. I'd forgotten my wind-up alarm clock, but wanted more than anything in the world to get up at 5:00 a.m. to go fishing. My folks let me take the old rowboat out into the cove by myself to fish, and the independence of taking a real boat out onto the water by myself was intoxication to an 11-year-old boy who loved to fish.

When I realized I had no way to wake at 5:00, I went to bed early with the hope that I'd wake early. However, the harder

I tried, the less able I was to fall asleep. It was past midnight when my folks finally turned in, the cabin went dark, and I finally found sleep.

The next thing I knew, I was wide awake. It was dark, and I could hear the sounds of the pre-dawn woods around me. I sat up and shone the flashlight on my watch. Lo and behold, it was straight-up 5:00! I quietly gathered my stuff, and made my way through the woods down to the boat as the sky above the trees began to gather a little light. I slipped the boat out onto the glassy surface of the water, and fished.

Later, at the breakfast table, nobody else seemed as amazed as I was that I woke up at exactly 5:00. It was a momentous discovery for me—the fact that I could will myself to wake at an exact time. To this day, if I fall asleep with a particular time I want to wake, I'll wake nearly to the minute of that time. Sadly, most mornings I'm waking up long before there's any real "reason" to wake up.

Like that morning all those years ago, the pre-dawn darkness sees me quietly stealing out into the wilderness, away from people, toward solitude. Rather than stealing through the woods down to the quiet mist rolling across a glassy lake, I roll down the road through a sleeping town toward the vast empty expanse of the Mojave Desert. Rather than the soft sound of water against the side of my tiny rowboat as I push it onto the surface of the water, I'm hearing the sweet sound of my freshly oiled chain reflected from the buildings in town as I push my bicycle out onto the surface of a vast desert wilderness.

Once I leave town, the next services are 90 miles east, the longest crossing I've ever made. My cache of water at the 70 mile mark is my insurance policy should the wind turn bad on me. In addition, I have two full water bottles, two liters of Gatorade, and another half-liter of water in a bladder stowed away in my bag.

This crossing brings me to within shouting distance of the threshold of mortality. If the wind blows the wrong direction, or the heat gets particularly high, I'll have a pretty tough day. If both happen, I could be in serious trouble—the kind of serious trouble that can be life-threatening.

Not to over-dramatize the risk. I am, after all, on a public highway. In most cases, if I end up in serious trouble, there's at least some chance that I can flag down help. Nonetheless, I'm alone on a bicycle crossing a desert wilderness in the summer. Things can turn ugly in a hurry.

So why on earth am I doing this? These next few days really are the "heart of the truth" for me, crossing first this Mojave, then the Sonoran. Crossing the heart of truth, out on the edge of comfort and safety.

> *Edge: A rim or a brink, or, a place where something*
> *is likely to begin. A penetrating and incisive quality,*
> *or, the degree of sharpness of an instrument designed*
> *to cut. Keenness, as of desire or enjoyment; zest: The*
> *brisk walk gave an edge to my appetite.*

(Compilation from several sources.)

•

Life happens on the edges. We can't find the next place on our journey until we discover the edge between the place we are and the place we need to go. Something ends and something else can begin only along an edge. Along these edges we find and feel the penetrating and incisive qualities that give definition to our life. Our interface with life is sharpened at the edge. We discover our greatest zest and our most keen desires at the edge.

I feel alive in a way we rarely get to feel alive in our safe and coddled culture today. Dawn spreads a beautiful pastel palette of color across the eastern horizon in front of me, adding fuel to my wonder and excitement.

Twenty miles out of town, I stop along the side of the road to take in a few calories and some liquid. The sun has crept above the horizon, a bright furnace of nuclear fusion, beginning the morning ascent into his throne in the sky. Mountains rim the horizon around me. The air is crystal clear. I'm a tiny dot in a vast petri dish of sand and desert plants.

And the silence . . .

The silence of the open desert again, that lack of *stuff* to create sound as the wind moves through it. A great metaphor for our time here in this life. While we're here, we might as well be invisible were it not for the impact we have on the world around us. The things we move through make the music that becomes our life.

Once we leave, the only thing we leave behind is the sound we made while moving through the obstacles we find. The only thing we take with us is the silence we've nurtured in our heart. We're like an invisible wind, only apparent to the universe around us through the deeds we do, the songs we sing, and the harmonies we create in the world as we move through it.

The hypnotic silence wraps itself around me. The early morning magic soaks into me as surely as the heat from the rising morning sun burns into my cheeks. I've always enjoyed the quiet, but am discovering a new dimension to silence here in the still desert morning. No cricket chirps, no bird sings, no leaves rustle with the movement of air. A truck drives by. I hear it coming from miles away, and hear it for miles as it moves down the highway after it passes. With every 50 or 60 seconds, it puts another mile between itself and me, and drops the sound even further.

Deep silence is something so rare that it's both conspicuous and remarkable when it confronts us. As I reflect into the depths of the silence around me, the desert itself becomes both more surreal and more personal. Quiet so deep and so broad that it becomes one of the prominent defining dimensions of the world around me. It's hypnotic. Mesmerizing. Sensual. I know I should get moving down the highway, but the silence holds me. I wallow in it.

12

MOJAVE TAILWIND

*The universe if full of magical things patiently
waiting for our wits to grow sharper.*

Eden Philpotts

GLIDING ACROSS THE DESERT

Heat is the other prominent dimension of the world around
me right now, and the reason I need to be making my way
down the highway. It's June in the desert. While it's barely
past sunup, it's blistering hot and becoming more so. I need to
move forward. Silence might be only the first of the wonders
this wilderness has to show me today.

The wind begins to move with the rising sun, pressing de-
lightfully against my back as I continue to make my way east
into the rising sun. The traffic remains extremely light, and the
few cars that do pass give me lots of room. The tailwind allows me to maintain a steady 20 miles per hour, gliding along
the highway with my head up and enjoying every morsel of
beautiful lonely desert I pass through.

The increasing wind blows sand along the desert floor,
creating a hazy and fuzzy effect in the distance, backdropped

by faraway mountains. Distance is hard to judge through the clear air above the ground haze of sand, adding yet another surreal dimension to the wilderness I'm gliding through.

Stopping to access more water from my pack, I gaze out across the sandy world to my east. I stand there quietly, in awe at what feels like the entire universe opening in front of me. The road descends in a gentle grade for the next ten miles or so, then the desert floor kicks upward, the road a tiny line etched onto its surface, disappearing in the distance. I stop and inhale the beauty of the scene for several minutes.

Climbing back into the saddle, I give myself to the road as it pulls me down the slope, the wind behind pushing me, a melody of happiness resonating from deep in my soul.

A joyful, sensual glide. I barely pedal at all, wanting the ride to last as long as possible. Sitting up straight in the saddle, no hands on the handlebars, weaving the bike gently back and forth down the highway, I drink in the delicious moment. Not a single car passes either way during the 30 minutes of descent. All the way down the slope, light singing and humming spills out of me as I savor one of the sweetest moments of riding I've ever experienced.

A few miles further up the road, I reach the junction with Highway 177 coming up from Desert Center to the south. I stop at this junction to munch on a granola bar and enjoy some water. Relaxing at the side of the road, I notice the heavier traffic on 177, realizing that I'll have a busier road to contend with now.

Several cars pull off where I'm sitting, taking pictures back along the road I just came across. It's a beautiful site. I hear snippets of conversations as doors open and somebody stands out of the car for a minute to snap the picture. The conversations include comments about how hot it is, followed by a "hurry up and get back in the car and close the door—you're letting all the air conditioning out."

Back safely in the glass and steel capsule, these folks don't need to worry about the heat as they crank their AC up to high, and turn the radio up to enjoy their favorite music. They escape from the wonderful silence that's been gently massaging my brain for the last few hours. They escape from the deep beauty of the desert wilderness.

They avoid an edge. They might see real life from that edge, but they retreat from it back into a capsule of glass, steel, and plastic.

It's been a little over a week since I came across this highway in a car. I remember stopping at this exact spot to admire the view. I enjoyed the view for a couple minutes, then climbed back in the car and drove along. I recognize the folks who're so anxious for the air conditioning; they are me on a different day and in a different state of mind.

I'm happy it's today, and I continue to revel in the state of mind that's wrapped itself around me.

At 70 miles, I stop and dig up my cache of water. While I could have made it to Vidal Junction without this cache, I'm quite happy to be able to drink as much as I want and fill my water bottles. On a day even hotter than today with a different wind, this water could have saved my life. Today it's a welcome convenience.

It's close to noon, and I eat another granola bar while I'm topping the water bottles. The intense heat from the sun is inescapable. I'd love a few minutes of shade if any were around. I'm wearing white in the desert to reflect as much of the heat as I can, but where the sun hits my arms and legs, the darker skin is converting quite a bit of that sunlight into heat. Wearing long sleeves and pant legs that were all white would be even smarter.

Twenty miles further up the road, I spend some time savoring the air conditioning and some ice cream at the little convenience store at Vidal Junction. The temperature reads 119. In the shade.

I roll into the motel in Parker, Arizona around 2:00 in the afternoon. After a warm shower and burrito dinner, I relax on a soft bed in the air conditioning. Today's been a particularly enjoyable day of cycling. I journeyed along a dangerous edge today, with nobody but me to depend on, and came out in good shape. Something grew within me today as I made my way along that edge. The tailwind was a bonus that turned this day of adventure into what might be the nicest day on a bicycle I've ever experienced in my life.

13

THE SONORAN

*I have always loved the desert. One sits down on
a desert sand dune, sees nothing, hears nothing. Yet
through the silence something throbs, and gleams . . .*
Antuine de Saint-Exupery, *The Little Prince*

DAY 9 • PARKER TO CONGRESS, ARIZONA

I'm up and riding at first light. There's more traffic today at
this early hour than I've been seeing, and I consider whether it
would have been wise to have a brighter headlight with me. I
started the trip with a brighter one, but that extra pound or two
was part of the flotsam I jettisoned back in Paso Robles. Sitting in the comfort of my living room, planning the trip out,
it seemed like an easy and obvious choice to bring along the
heavy extra light in order to add another level of security to
my morning rides. However, out where the rubber and the road
come together, the scales took on a different tilt.

It's easy to talk about the abstract notion of security. We'd
all like to feel completely and totally secure, to feel that no danger can touch us. From the time we're infants, we reach for the
arms of our mothers, where nothing can harm us or scare us.

But life can be a dangerous place. The deeper we bury ourselves under the weight of security, the less *real life* is available for us to live. Every form of security has a price, and too often, we simply accept that added security is the highest priority. It's so easy to do. We get scared, and we want the scared to go away. We never stop reaching for mother's arms.

But should security really be our priority? Always? Is safety the highest priority in life, the thing we want the most? On our deathbed, do we want to proclaim that, above all else, we remained safe?

What's the risk, and what's the cost to mitigate it? Those are the questions. Life doesn't give us the luxury of eliminating every risk, or living in a perfectly secure environment. Life extracts a price for every risk we mitigate. We've got to be smart enough to mitigate wisely. At some point, we need to let go of mom's arms, and face the risks life has to offer us. That's the only way to discover real life.

That's living.

Helen Keller said that security is mostly a superstition, that it doesn't exist in nature. She said that life is either a grand adventure or nothing at all.

I'll choose grand adventure every time.

.

It's hot even before the sun breaks the horizon, rising sharp and bright on my left, casting my shadow off across the desert to my right. For those first few minutes, my shadow seems to stretch all the way to the distant mountains, before the rising sun draws it back toward me.

I love sunrise. Heck, I just love early morning in general. But sunrises are quite special. They each take on their own complexion. Kansas sunrises are generally different from Ohio sunrises. Sunrise in Cambodia is different from both.

A desert sunrise announces the arrival of a powerful lord, one that can be malevolent and terrible. While the sight is beautiful, it pours tremendous power and heat down onto me from the moment it cracks the horizon. The sun is barely above the horizon, and I feel that heat poured over me like hot wax.

At about 15 miles, the road forks. Most of the traffic stays on 95 headed south, while I remain on 72 and head southeast. I welcome the return to desolation.

The low eastern sun has already cranked the heat of the desert up to a low broil as I roll into the little town of Bouse. Filling my water bottles and taking in a few calories, I chat with a few folks. They're a good sight short of friendly, though not downright hostile. It could be that folks in the town don't see many outsiders and don't cotton to them, or it could be that they think I'm some sort of crazy man riding a bicycle in the middle of the desert in June. Or it could be that the three people I talk to just happen to be in a bad mood today.

Every year in June, the RAAM (Race Across America) occurs. It's a totally insane bicycle race from San Diego to Annapolis. Coast to coast, nonstop. Everybody leaves San Diego together, and the first guy to Annapolis wins. *These* guys are truly off their rockers, riding 20 plus hours a day. The winner usually makes it in about 9 days. Really. Look it up. This really happens. (For more information on the annual Race Across America, check out their website at www.raceacrossamerica, view a great documentary called *Bicycle Dreams* by Stephen Auerbach.)

Yesterday, I connected with the route the RAAM follows on its journey across America. I'm about a week or so in front of those guys as they race this year, and I'm curious about the impact the race has on these small towns it goes through. I ask the guy at the store about the race, and he seems to understand that some big bicycle thing happens, but doesn't know much about it. This seems crazy to me; it must be the single biggest thing that happens to this tiny little town each year, and this guy is only vaguely aware of it? Surely he can't be a shop owner who profits from the event?

An old fella sitting outside has found a little corner of shade. I lean against the building close to where he's sitting, and throw out a couple "small talk" conversation starters. He's just not feelin' much like talking, or he takes a long time to warm up to a conversation. After three or four tries at engaging the guy in the smallest of talk, I give up, wish him a nice day, and climb back into the saddle, headed out into the broiling morning sun.

The desert has taken on a new complexion this morning. Riding further south and east, the landscape around me is dotted with saguaro cactus, while the sandy landscape beneath the saguaro is covered only thinly with desert plants. The saguaro are fascinating, standing regal and tall, welcoming the heat and desiccation, an endless army of green soldiers scattered across the desert for as far as the eye can see, soaking in all the punishment the sledgehammer sun can pour down on them.

The saguaro blooms from April to June. I'm at the very end of the bloom. The beautiful white flowers are out in full force this morning, shining brilliantly in the bright sunlight. Many of them have turned to a ruby colored fruit. I ponder the adaptability of life as I pedal through the heat, appreciating this plant that grows and blooms and produces fruit out here in such a hostile environment.

I'm feeling pretty small in this desert. This *shrinking* may have been developing slowly as I've come deeper into deserts, but I'm acutely aware of the feeling this morning. The brilliant dish of blue above me reflects across the vast expanse of sandy landscape around me. On most sides, along the horizon, mountains form the rim of the desert.

I'm the tiniest of specks on this vast desert, dwarfed by giant saguaro that stand 20 and 30 feet tall on all sides of me. Indeed, a firmament above and a firmament below, language borrowed from some other desert folk. Looking at the world around me, the language makes perfect sense this morning.

Traffic is sparse. A light quartering headwind keeps me company all the way to the end of Highway 72 at the junction with Highway 60, where I turn left. I stop and take in the last of my water, realizing that I'm at a significant turn here. I've traveled 700 miles so far, meandering generally southeast since I started back in Monterey. This marks the southernmost point on my trip. With this left turn, I'll begin a northeast bearing that will move me back toward Colorado, at which point I'll continue east.

I would have expected to feel "homeward bound" at this point, with a corresponding excitement. More cogent is my sense of sadness while crossing this milestone, signifying the passing of so much of the trip. I'm enjoying the peace and harmony I'm discovering in the deep solitude this trip is bringing to me. I'm feeling strong as my body comes into a high level of fitness that deals well with the long days of riding. The moments I'm traveling through become more enjoyable with each passing mile.

Life is very good. I'm happy. Content. Alone, but not lonely.

A friend once said to me, "you must be really comfortable in your own skin." We were discussing the fact that I often enjoyed hunting trips alone, where I'd camp and hunt by myself for several days at a time. He's a very social person, and said that so much time with nobody else around would drive him crazy.

It's true I suppose. I am comfortable in my own skin. While I enjoy being around other people, I also truly enjoy time I spend on my own. By myself, I'm able to find a more intense quality of thought than I can when I feel others around me. In solitude, the depth of my reflection grows. Spending energy interacting with others reduces the energy available for introspection, inspection, contemplation and speculation.

14

DESERT DEVIL DANCERS

*Language . . . has created the word 'loneliness' to
express the pain of being alone. And it has created
the word 'solitude' to express the glory of being alone.*

Paul Johannes Tillich, *The Eternal Now*

SENSUAL SAND

The road surface along Highway 60 is outstanding. The wide
and well-maintained shoulder leads me to expect heavy traffic
that never develops. The heat seems to build with every pedal
stroke. An intense heat that rolls across me and pulls the moisture from me faster than I can replace it.

Stopping at a convenience store in Salome for calories
and liquid, I enjoy the respite of some delicious AC, a welcome
contrast to the absurd heat outside. I talk to the owner about
the upcoming RAAM, and she's very aware of it. The race or-
ganizers have already been on the phone with her to confirm
the hours she'll be open, and it's an event she looks forward to
each year. This is the reaction I'd expected from someone who
can profit from the event while providing much-needed services.

The store is quintessential small-town America. Mom runs the store, grandma is there watching after the small kids. Everybody who walks in the front door knows everybody else, and town gossip flows richly. In 20 minutes, I learn more than my share about several folks in town, just listening to the conversations around the front counter.

Walking out of the store with full water bottles and sated thirst, the heat descends on me and drenches me. I'm a little nervous about whether my two bottles of water will be enough to make it 30 miles to Aguila, and walk back in to buy a little more liquid to be safe. Back in the saddle and pedaling down the road, there's a surrealistic quality to the flat road stretching out in front of me along the hot desert floor. A perfectly straight line of dark asphalt, disappearing into a cloud of shimmering heat far away in the miles ahead of me. Now and then, appearing magically from within this bright amorphous blanket across the road, a car will come toward me on the highway. As a car passes me going in my direction, I watch as they travel away from me and disappear into that magical shimmering cloud.

Saguaro cactus stand sentry throughout the sparse vegetation on both sides of the road, clumps of velvet mesquite in the low spots and washes. Along with the clumps of bright white flowers on the saguaro are holes drilled high up on the bigger ones. I assume the holes are home to the small finch-type birds I see moving around on the plants occasionally. As the afternoon progresses, the beautiful white saguaro flowers wilt, surrendering to the oppressive heat.

Far off on the vast plane of desolation to my left, sand and dust formed by the wind rises into a swirling dance across the desert. The little "storms" remind me of tornadoes, though there's no "top" to them. They swirl from a narrow point on the ground up into a funnel of sand that rises toward the sky, where the funnel just ends. I suspect the air currents go higher, but the "top" I see is just the highest point that the swirling wind carries the sand from the desert floor before dropping it again, the falling sand creating a haze around the base of the funnels. In the Midwest, we call these dust devils, but I've never seen one that remotely approaches the scale of these I'm watching.

Several of these devils spin gracefully across the distant desert. Like a troupe of exotic dancers, weaving their way across the desert expanse, singing a seductive visual song across the miles, a song made more sensual by the heat pressing all around me. The silence around me adds a bass harmony, completed by the high harmony of the surreal cloud at the end of the distant ribbon of asphalt spitting cars toward me while swallowing the cars moving away from me. I'm reminded again how often mystics seem to wander in the desert.

15

COYOTE FLATS

What makes the desert beautiful is that
somewhere it hides a well.

Antoine de Saint-Exupery

WHAT, EXACTLY, DID I EXPECT?

I have a constitution that does well in the heat. Folks around me will surrender to it and seek the respite of air conditioning or the shade before I do. Part of this is because I'm bald, so my body can lose a lot of heat quickly. (A "feature" that quickly becomes a "defect" when winter comes along, by the way.) But part of it's just due to how I seem to be put together. My body just stays cooler than most.

But today, pedaling along the black asphalt under a sledgehammer desert sun, the heat is rapidly draining the energy from me. I've struggled all day to stay hydrated and I'm losing that battle. In these conditions, you just can't keep enough water going into your system to replace what's evaporating off your skin. I'd really like to find a place to relax and get out of the heat, but the bright expanse of sand and rock offers no refuge.

It's June in the Sonoran Desert, what did you expect? the desert seems to whisper.

Eventually, the highway crosses a dry wash with mesquite hanging over the shoulder. Dragging my bike with me, I crawl under the thorny branches, seeking the shade that's hiding there. Huddled in the little scrap of shade beneath the mesquite, I finish the last of my water, but can't stomach the idea of a dry granola bar.

In Aquila, the Coyote Flats Cafe and Bar sings a sweet invitation to me as it comes into view. I lean my bike against the window in the cool shade beneath a big awning. Leaving my helmet and gloves with the bike, I saunter through the front door, me and my Lycra. What's it like, you might wonder, sauntering into a desert bar called "Coyote Flats" wrapped in Lycra? Looking back, it does seem a little odd. But the only thing on my mind as I walk through the front door is water and cool air.

The place is mostly empty, just one couple in a booth behind me as I sit at the bar. I order water, a pitcher of it, straight up, eliciting the faintest of smiles from the waitress. She's an attractive gal with enough miles on the odometer to know the gas pedal from the brake pedal, and has no interest in flirting with the weird old guy in spandex who just walked into the bar.

I've put down half a pitcher of water by the time she comes to take my order. She fills another pitcher and sets it in front of me, standing with her pen in her hand, distracted, waiting for me to order. It's early afternoon and well north of 100 degrees. Perusing the menu, I comment on the heat. "Man, it's hot out there."

Setting her order pad down on the counter, crossing her arms, tapping the back of her pen against her lower lip, she looks out the window at my bike leaning there. Her eyes drift to mine with that look women can give men. You know the look, the one that says, "I'm wondering if you're trying to act dumb, or if you really might be that dumb." Not necessarily mean, just curious.

I smile sheepishly beneath the pressure of the question

behind her look. Every man reading these words knows exactly what I'm talking about here. You get the look, so you know you've said or done something really stupid, but you don't have a clue what it is you've done or said that is so outrageously idiotic. Which just makes it worse.

She sees all this wash across my face, and a small smile plays at the corners of her face. Still tapping the pen against her lower lip, she brings her elbows down to rest on the bar, leaning in a little closer to me, as if letting me in on her secret. "Honey, it's June. It's the hottest month in the Sonoran Desert." Pausing, she looks again at my bicycle leaning against her window. "You're riding a bicycle across the black asphalt in the hottest desert in the hottest month."

She pauses there, looking into my eyes, raising one eyebrow, letting me know a question is coming. "What, exactly, did you expect?"

Hmmm. Good point. I might have heard those words whispered to me by the desert itself earlier today.

"Right," I say, closing the menu and handing it to her, keeping my eyes on hers. "I'll take the burger." We smile at each other as she takes the menu.

The final 25 miles of the day follows Highway 71 up to Congress. While I've seen either a headwind or a crosswind for most of the day, I enjoy a tailwind for this final section. A tailwind is a welcome bonus, but I don't enjoy it as much as I should. I gain about 1000 feet over this stretch, the asphalt is hot, and I'm suffering more than a little from the heat. One of the few times in my life when I feel like a tailwind is wasted on me.

Heat on asphalt is an interesting thing for the cyclist. When the temperature gets over 100, the black asphalt absorbs enough heat that it softens up a bit. It's not something you notice in a car, but if you look at the highway, you'll see evidence of it in the ruts left on asphalt where truck tires pass. The truck tires are carrying a lot more weight per square inch of rubber on the ground, so they sink in more noticeably.

On a bicycle with narrow tires, you notice it. Peddling gets just a little harder, like you're always going up a little grade. Late on this hot day, the asphalt has softened up, adding just a bit more work for my last 25 miles of the day, pushing me that much further past the edge of comfort.

The threshold of comfort is generally closer than we think. We like a nice 75 degree day, with enough humidity to stay comfortable. In the "big scale" of possible temperatures (the Kelvin scale), 75 degrees Fahrenheit is 296.888 degrees Kelvin. Add 35 degrees Fahrenheit to that to put us over the precipice and into the danger zone for survival at 110 degrees Fahrenheit, and we have 316.333 degrees Kelvin. The difference is only about 6 percent. The difference between the perfect temperature and deadly heat is only 6 percent.

We've found ways to live our entire lives within that narrow band of comfort, separated from deadly peril by a mere 6 percent. We live so exclusively within that narrow band of comfort that most of us never need to touch anything approaching the edge of that 6 percent buffer.

The human mind is wonderful it its ability to make the universe fit neatly into our comfort zone, ignoring everything beyond that zone. How different would our lives be if we could allow our minds and our souls to reach out beyond our zone of comfort? How far beyond comfort do we need to go to see and feel what we can't yet understand?

I'm overheated and parched dry as I pedal into the town of Congress, which feels like an oasis just now. My body wants a cool shower, plenty of fluid, and rest. Rolling up to the Sierra Vista Motel, I'm delighted beyond words to be done for the day.

The motel is run by a gal named Cindy, who once lived in Colorado herself. She's about my age, and might have been a bit of a hippie once. We share some great conversation, then I make my way to my room and enjoy a cool shower.

After my shower I head off in search of food, and, bonus of bonuses, 200 yards from the motel is the best meal I'll have on the entire trip, a little place called Nichols West, run by a fellow named Simon. He and his wife had a restaurant in New York City and decided to lease the property out and move to Arizona. By any standards anywhere on earth, their restaurant here is outstanding. If I lived in Phoenix, I'd drive to Congress just to eat at this place.

Now, I'd have felt great with the cool shower at the Sierra Vista Motel and the bonus of a world-class meal at Nichols West. But to top it off, a local guy sitting at the bar was talking politics with Simon. I join in the conversation and have a truly wonderful back and forth with the guy about the state of the nation and the world. We don't solve any problems, but I'm truly grateful to have someone to talk politics with. Maybe some folks would call it *argue politics*, but I think we both had a good time and learned a little something from each other. We buy each other a beer, and shake hands out by his truck as we part and go our separate ways.

Here's yet another bonus of finding joy and comfort in solitude. It brings me joy to be energized by moments of good human interaction between those moments of deep solitude. I'm truly grateful to this fellow for engaging in real conversation with me about real and important topics. We might have disagreed on many things, but that doesn't make either of us an idiot, it just means we disagree, both of us full of good intention. Real understanding of complex issues isn't easy. It takes mental energy. Discussing complex issues with others requires both mental and emotional energy.

Most of all, coming to real understanding of complex issues means you've got to be willing to get a little closer to the edge of that 6 percent comfort zone—out there where making sense of things takes both courage and intelligence. Here in little Congress, Arizona, I've found two new friends more than willing to mix it up a bit: Cindy at the Sierra Vista and my new best friend at the bar. What was his name again?

Sedona, AZ

Congress, AZ

SCRUB OAK
PONDEROSA

AND SEDONA

16

MINGUS PASS

There is pleasure in the pathless woods,
There is rapture on the lonely shore,
There is society where none intrudes,
By the deep sea and the music in its roar;
I love not man the less, but Nature more.

Lord Byron

DAY 10 • CONGRESS TO SEDONA, ARIZONA

I expected to enjoy the solitude of my ride, and I have. More than I'd anticipated. The desert amplifies solitude. Wandering across these deserts has moved me beyond my expectations. I've found a deeper peace within myself.

How does the desert do this? I've always enjoyed time on my own. In solitude I've been able to discover the things within me and about me that make me what I am today. Time spent alone has always inspirited my mind and my soul, opening me up to myself. But this time alone through the desert has been teaching me a new dimension to solitude.

It started the morning I rode out of Twentynine Palms to cross the Mojave, after 20 miles when I stopped to take in water and food. Leaning against my bike with the low morning sun on my shoulder, the sacredness of the moment, the silence, the depth of the vast desolation. It was palpable. I could see for dozens of miles all around me. Even when the land was rising in one direction or the other, it rose with a constancy that accentuated the immensity of the openness around me. The silence and vastness were stunning.

I'd started to see bits of this on previous days of riding as I was moving into the Mojave, but that moment east of Twentynine Palms it consumed me. I could *feel* the hallowed wilderness pulling me into itself.

Solitude always wraps me in the inescapable arms of *self-ness*. The desert solitude I've discovered is much larger and deeper. It's wrapped me and the silence around me into itself. I'm swallowed by the desert around me. The arms of solitude pull the desert through me and me through the desert. Is it introspection still, or is it something different? Extrospection?

I'd been learning about myself in a wider classroom. I'm a piece of a powerful wilderness around me, a wilderness that's both merciless in its deadliness and profound in its beauty.

I feel these thoughts as I roll out of Congress before dawn the next morning, listening to the sweet sound of my spinning chain bounce off the dark and silent buildings. Only a tiny hint of light rims the eastern sky. Dawn, this sweetest moment of the day. It's just me and the wonder of the world around me.

Dawn seeps into the eastern sky across my right shoulder as I pedal northeast on Highway 89. The first five miles is open and big, allowing me to enjoy the glory of the growing light around me. Traffic is light as I climb the gentle grade, and I can see the climbing is going to get more serious up the road a ways. By the time I hit the steeper grade, I'm warmed up and ready for the work.

The climb is glorious. With no traffic and two good lanes in each direction, a great shoulder is a bonus. As I climb, the sunrise unfolds to my right. The new day's golden light spills onto the desert below. I'm a bit sad to be leaving the desert, and at the same time, happy to be climbing to a cooler elevation that will take me through landscape and plant-life a lot like my high prairie home in Colorado.

Cresting the climb, I glide down through the little town of Yarnell, after which I enjoy some gentle rolling terrain for 10 miles or so. By the time I reach Wilhoit and see continued climbing in my future, the wind has picked up and pounds across me from the right. Seeing no evidence of a real diner, I stop at a little grocery on the right as I come into town.

Walking outside with an armload of food and drink, I head toward a picnic table in the shade. A group of local older fellas sits around the table, telling stories and talking hunting, fishing, and politics. They seem eager for some new blood at their table as I wander up and ask if I can join them. It's like the "big table" at the local small-town diner at breakfast time, but there's no diner, and it's just a broken-down picnic table. Still, it's the local guys chewin' the fat together in the shade.

A lot of cyclists stay aloof from the people around them as they cycle. All the spandex and crazy jerseys we wear make us look different from anyone else on the planet. I turn off self-consciousness in most cases, and ignore what I might look like. Walking up to a bunch of redneck looking guys sitting around a table in the shade in a rural setting is something most cyclists would avoid, and these guys might even be a little shocked by this spandex-clad thing with an armload of food sitting down at the table with them.

These are not the droids you're looking for . . .

We sit and chat for quite a while. Generally, these guys are retired or trying to retire, and live in trailers close by. (That ultimate of redneck cabins, the Double Wide . . .) I ask about the road ahead of me toward Sedona, and am amazed at the different stories I get. Seems few of them actually drive it, but one old fellow talks a lot about these big climbs and valleys and more climbs. I figure he must be wrong since that's just not how I'm picturing it. My picture of the road ahead is mostly flat over to Prescott, then a long easy descent into Sedona. Surely I know more about the road in front of me than these guys . . . The confabulation breaks up after 45 minutes, and we shake hands and head our separate ways. They've got stuff to do, and I've got a little riding in front of me. Surely, once I climb over to Prescott, I'll be done with the climbing for the day, and can enjoy a nice gentle slope down into Sedona. Surely the one guy is confused about all that climbing between here and there . . .

After a few miles of climbing, a winding descent draws me down into Prescott. The mountains here feel like home to me, and the cool air is a delightful change from the desert.

In Prescott I stop at Ironclad Bicycles, and get a new chain put on my bike. The guys at the shop are friendly and helpful, and we chat about touring as they work on my bike. I ask them about the ride over to Sedona, and they talk about a big pass I'll need to cross, and several miles of long false flat that's always brutally windy.

Hmmm. Maybe the old guy in Wilhoit knew more than I gave him credit for. Still, it's probably not as windy or steep as this guy is making out.

Funny the way our brains work. I get a picture in my mind of the way things are and I'm very slow to give it up, even in the face of strong contrary evidence. Especially when I like the picture I've got in my mind. This morning, I started out with a mental picture of the day's ride. I have solid first-hand testimony from folks who live here and drive and ride these roads that the picture in my mind is wrong. Yet, I hang on to this picture.

Looking back on history, it seems this is just how we work. As the dawn of modern thinking was breaking across the Middle Ages, European thinkers had what they believed to be an accurate picture of the universe in their minds. There was this firmament above and this firmament below, waters above and waters below, and that's the way the universe was constructed. Thinkers from more advanced cultures (Arabs and Mongols) brought ideas and evidence into Europe suggesting that maybe the earth wasn't a flat plate.

Hundreds of years went by before the crazy notion of a spherical earth was accepted by those in power in Europe, and once they accepted it, their comfortable perspective began immediately to be invaded by the crazy notion that the earth might not be the center of the universe. Galileo and others paid a steep price before the minds of those in power finally bent to accept what many others had accepted for close to 2000 years.

It's just how we're put together. We hang on to old constructs at all costs. We resist new ideas. We resist any challenge to the accuracy of the picture we've got painted in our minds. In many ways, I have this "conservative" mindset. There's both good and bad in this, and I need to balance things as I move through life. One of the "less good" things about a conservative mindset is hanging on to old constructs much longer than I should . . .

It's early afternoon as I pedal out of Prescott after a fine lunch from an old west saloon. My stubborn conservative mindset comes face-to-face with that radical wind the guys back at the bicycle shop were warning me about as I ascend the long false flat they described so well. The brutal wind blowing across me consumes my concentration and saps my capacity for joy. The road curves into a slowly steepening climb that draws me into the folds of the mountains, offering some respite from the howling wind.

The climb up to Mingus Pass is a gorgeous 10 miles. The road is decent and the traffic reasonable. The guys at the bike shop said the descent was long and steep, so I'm looking forward to a screaming downhill reward after the climb.

It's an understatement to describe the view from the top of Mingus out toward Sedona and Cottonwood as stunning. It's truly postcard material, though I suspect this is one of those pictures that can't be expressed well in a photograph. Like the Grand Canyon. Pictures look picturesque, but you have to stand there to really feel the scope of the world your eyes are taking in.

The screamin' downhill on the other side isn't much of a reward after all. It's very steep indeed, very narrow, with sharp turns and a terrible road surface. I'm on the brakes for so long that at one point I pull over to the side just to rest from the braking.

Coming into the little town of Jerome, I'm reminded of riding through little towns in the mountains of Italy. The buildings and homes are built into the mountainside as you switchback around them on the narrow street. I have an immediate, strong, and pleasant memory of a long ride with my son Ian one day in northern Italy several years ago.

Jerome is an old mining town that has been restored into a quaint little touristy place. I've been out of water since the top of Mingus Pass, and I'm a little worried about where my next place to get water might be, since I'm not passing any gas stations or convenience stores in town. A lady on the sidewalk assures me there's a gas station a couple miles down the road, so I keep going.

From Jerome it's a wonderful glide on good road down to Clarkdale. I'm able to finally fly at a delightful 50 miles per hour without squeezing the brakes, drinking in the exhilaration. I drink a tremendous amount of water and fill my bottles at the gas station, then continue down the road into Cottonwood.

At Cottonwood, the elevation hits another low point, and I start a climb for the last 20 miles to Sedona. While I gain a thousand feet, I have a wonderful tailwind, and feel like Superman powering rapidly along the highway. I've ridden over a hundred miles for the day, and the temperature is back up over 100, but the beauty of the high desert unfolding around me fills me with energy that the miles and heat had beat out of me just a short time ago.

I arrive bone weary at my old friend Dale's doorstep in Sedona thirteen hours after starting my day back down the road in Congress. My expectations for the day were thoroughly trounced, and those crushed expectations wore me out more than the 110 miles and 9,000 feet of climbing.

Arriving at Dale's house, he's clearly not feeling well. He says he has a virus. We chat briefly about old times, pulling me up out of the weariness I'd been wallowing in, and Dale says he's feeling better as well. A cool shower washes any remaining fatigue from me, and we go out and enjoy some dinner together.

17

SEDONA

There is a voice that doesn't use words. Listen.

Rumi

DAY 11 • DALE

Dale is both an old friend and a former boss. A guy known for his hard-hitting personality and relentlessly demanding style, Dale never approached anything obliquely. Everything was a straight-on route for Dale, the most direct path from point A to point B.

While I like a direct approach, I often prefer a more oblique strategy to solving problems, coming at them from a couple different angles to understand them better. This difference in our styles was apparent in our careers as well, as I've wandered off on sideways paths more than once.

Sometimes Dale's manner worked better in business, sometimes mine, but between us we solved a lot of problems. Together, and with the help of some excellent co-workers, we built his companies into a tiny empire, taking him to a point of excellent financial success, the "point B" he had always sought. When it comes to building wealth and empire, a direct and single-minded approach is hard to beat.

I, on the other hand, had gone off chasing sideways pathways and ideas: a route that's excellent for collecting eclectic experiences, but not so great for building wealth and empire. When I left Dale and his companies, we parted as good friends. A couple years after I left he sold his companies and became very financially secure. Well, wealthy, really.

I was busy exploring oblique little pathways . . .

We've maintained our friendship over these many years. Though Dale and I fought many battles when we worked together, and were often in serious conflict, we always respected one-another. This respect is what carried our friendship over past the day I left him and his company.

I planned the route of this trip so I could stop and take this rest day in Sedona with Dale, and I've been looking forward to it. It's been years since we got to spend relaxed time together.

Dale is a perfect host, and takes me on a tour of all the sites in Sedona. I meet some of the folks that he's building his "retired" life around in Sedona, which is a very different life than he maintained while he was building his companies. We enjoy steaks out on his back patio at the end of the day, along with some of the best conversation I've ever had with Dale.

When we're young men, in the prime of our strength and vigor, we tend to have a bit of fire in our bellies. With some folks it's a hotter fire than others. With men at least, this fire burns pretty hot in our 20s and 30s, before starting the slow cooling process in our 40s or 50s. This fire drives us to be quick to analyze things, quick to draw judgments, quick to make decisions. We're always moving forward, and we need to move forward rapidly. Damn the torpedoes, we've got war to wage, problems to solve, mountains to move.

With Dale, that fire was hot when he was a young man. He's about 10 years older than me, so we're close enough in age that while we often disagreed about how to wage whatever battle we were fighting, we always fought the battles back-to-back and with a gleam in our eyes.

Dale's tendency to be critical and judgmental about others has always bothered me. Truth be told, I suspect I've sometimes had the same tendency, and he probably found that same quality in me just as bothersome. I imagine we just judged different things, and in different ways. Perhaps it was simply an unfortunate part of our nature as young men.

But the Dale I enjoy supper with on his back patio tonight is one I never knew in those earlier days of battle and glory. He's thoughtful and deliberate in his thinking. He clearly works to see many perspectives of something. He's very sure of himself, but in a way dramatically different from the way of a young man.

As young men, we cover our insecurity with a facade of boldness and assurance, causing us to draw rapid judgments with which we color our world. It helps us create the sense of stability we need to wage our battles. As we collect years, we get better at finding the battles that really matter. A deeper and more true sense of confidence and security grows within us, and we become more comfortable with who we are and our place in the world. We develop the courage to open our minds a bit, and see other colors with which the world might be painted.

It's an interesting irony that the more comfortable and secure I am with myself, my place in the world, and my belief, the more open I am to hearing and understanding folks who might have a viewpoint that differs from mine.

Dale has collected years well, and we talk for hours about a wide range of topics. Often, he does an outstanding job of articulating a position that I know he doesn't necessarily agree with, but he nonetheless cares enough to understand a converse position fully and express it well.

I always refer to Dale as one of my greatest mentors. Not that I did everything as he suggested; in fact, most of what I learned from him I probably rejected. But some of my most important lessons in business I learned from Dale. In this new Dale sitting across the table from me, I see qualities worth emulating, and hope I collect years as well as he has.

We clean up the dishes and load my bicycle into the trunk

of Dale's Cadillac for an early start in the morning. He has emphatically insisted he wants to drive me north out of Sedona in the early morning. He's worried about the narrow switchbacks I'll have to climb. I assure tell him that I've been riding on some narrow and winding roads and that I'll be okay, but this is clearly something he wants to do. And really, missing some steep and dangerous switchbacks early in the morning twilight doesn't sound all that terrible to me.

Before going to sleep, I walk out of my bedroom into the cool air on the patio, reflecting on the changes I see in my friend Dale. Like good whiskey, many of us mellow with age. I have no doubt that I've mellowed a good deal as I've collected a few more years in the cask. I find Dale is no exception to this, and this more mellow and thoughtful Dale is a joy to be around. I hope age mellows me in ways as sweetly as it's mellowed Dale.

DAY 11 · SEDONA TO TUBA CITY, ARIZONA

We're up at 4:30 the next morning, headed up toward Flagstaff. There are a few miles of very narrow road indeed, and I can see why Dale was concerned. Reaching the top, I point out places where we can stop so Dale can drop me off, but he's clearly intent on taking me further.

The bulk of this drive is good road through pretty country on a beautiful morning, road I'd rather be riding my bike on. Not to mention the little tiny voice in my mind telling me this is a bicycle trip, not a car trip. But I realize that this ride is a demonstration of affection by Dale. He's worried about me riding on the narrow and steep portion of road, and he wants to give me something. This ride is that something. A couple times yesterday, I'd told Dale how much I appreciated the opportunities he gave me, and shared with him some regrets I had from those old days. During those conversations, Dale hadn't replied with any similar sentiments, but I could see thoughts and sentiments working behind his eyes.

This ride this morning is his way of expressing those appreciations and those sentiments. When this understanding strikes me, I sit back and tell him just how much I'm enjoying the ride.

And I smile.

Reaching the outskirts of Flagstaff, Dale pulls into an empty parking lot. I unload my bike, and strap my bag on the back. We exchange pleasantries, a long and strong handshake, and a slap on the back. Then Dale drives off. I watch as he pulls out of the parking lot, and heads south toward Sedona. Our short time together has been a delight; I hope to be able to see him again soon.

But fate has something else in mind, and Dale's life will come to an end in a few short weeks at the hands of a nasty but hidden infection that's working in his body even as we've had this wonderful time together.

Every handshake we have with a good friend could be the last. Every time we watch as they drive off could be our last glimpse. Each time we break bread with someone we love might be the last chance we get to do so.

My final chance to break bread with Dale was the finest, most insightful, and most enjoyable dinner I ever had with him. Our final handshake was strong and carried great affection. It came at the end of a relaxing early morning car ride that was Dale's way of saying thanks. I was smiling as I watched him drive away.

Rest in peace my friend, and thanks again for the ride!

THE RES

18

SOLITUDE LOST, FRIENDSHIP FOUND

Let us be grateful to people who make us happy, they are the charming gardeners who make our souls blossom.

Marcel Proust

FINDING DAVE

Dale turns his Cadillac toward his home, and I turn my bicycle toward Flagstaff. My good friend Dave drove out to Arizona from Colorado a couple days ago, making his way up from Phoenix on his bicycle, to Flagstaff where we've agreed to meet. We'll continue riding together from here to Kansas. We've ridden a lot together, and I'm looking forward to sharing time on the road with him.

Making my way to a Village Inn on the east side of Flagstaff where we've agreed to meet, I enjoy breakfast while waiting for Dave to arrive. The nature of my trip will change this morning from a journey of solitude to a shared journey with a good friend. While the solitude of the trip so far has been a sublime experience, I'm almost giddy with anticipation to see my good friend, and be able to share the joys of this trip with him.

Dave orders breakfast when he arrives, and we relax in the booth while he describes a young fellow on a bicycle he passed along the interstate this morning. The guy was riding a heavy duty touring bike loaded to the gills with anything he might need to survive out in the wilderness. While Dave and I carry well under 20 pounds of gear apiece, he figures this guy's gear had to weigh in at something north of 75 pounds.

This immediately opens up great breakfast conversation between us about the contrast between our minimalist style, and the more common fully loaded style of touring. It also opens up good discussion about the pros and cons of riding on different types of roads. It's a conversation we've wandered through many times, exploring the difference in our points of view on the subject. While Dave likes a quiet road more, he generally will argue for using an interstate highway when possible and legal. The shoulder is massive, allowing you to keep a good distance between you and the traffic. They're generally straight without steep climbs. They're efficient. He makes a strong argument for that point of view. From my perspective, I'll give up efficiency if it helps me avoid the traffic noise, the fumes, and all the glass, metal and other crap that litters the shoulder. If I have 500 square feet of space, would I rather pour a concrete slab, or plant a garden? Concrete is more efficient, takes less care, and is cheaper in the long run. The garden brings beauty to the space, and joy that can nourish the soul. It's a balance that requires an understanding of where the space is, who'll use it, and for what. We all bring our own bias to the balance, some of us leaning toward heartless efficiency, some of us leaning toward oblivious joy. Not that Dave or I are either heartless or oblivious. I lean a little toward the heart, Dave leans a little toward the mind, and we keep each other in balance.

It's metaphoric discussion territory for us, and we both smile as our banter falls so quickly into the space we enjoy with each other. Efficiency on the one hand, joy on the other, and finding the right balance of the two.

The road headed north out of Flagstaff is two lanes in each direction with a great shoulder. While it's fairly busy, it's not nearly as busy as the interstate. A gentle climb takes us up into wonderful Ponderosa Pine country that reminds me of home in Colorado. At a couple points, I catch the smell of elk. It's pretty strong in one spot, so I stop and scan the Ponderosa upwind of me. A couple hundred yards up the hill, a small group of them rests on the edge of dark timber, the sight bringing a *homey* feeling to my heart.

Back in the saddle and pedaling up the hill, the road crests at about 7500 feet, followed by a long and gentle drop out of the higher altitude with pines and shrub, and back into the high desert of northern Arizona. I enjoy the long descent sitting up high in the saddle, hands off the handlebars.

After lunch in Cameron at a spot that can only be described as a monument to tourist traps, we saddle up and continue north on 89. The traffic is heavy, and we're now down to two lanes with a marginal shoulder. About 20 miles north of Cameron we turn right on US 160, which will be our highway from here through most of Kansas on our journey east.

For the next three days, we'll be crossing the land of the Navaho, Hopi, and Ute. Rust-colored desert and bright red rocks sculpted into magical shapes create an otherworldly landscape around us. It's breathtaking at times. I can't imagine moving through this place and not feeling magic all around. How many places like this can there be on earth?

We're dodging more debris and glass on the shoulder, and this seems to be getting worse the deeper we move into Reservation lands. Why is this? Does the state highway budget not include maintenance of this highway because it passes through reservation land? I find it hard to believe that as the highway crosses the border into the Reservation, the drivers suddenly start throwing more stuff out their windows. After all, it's clear that the vast majority of the traffic along the road is "passing through"—the same traffic that was on the highway before it entered reservation land.

In my lifetime, I've experienced the beginning of an epic transformation in our cultural ethic on how we treat our environment. When I was a very young boy, it was common and widely accepted to throw trash out of the car window. When we were out fishing, my dad and uncle would leave their beer cans out in the lake. My uncle was a forestry officer, having what at the time was probably an elevated ethic on land use. He insisted they fill the empty cans with water so they'd sink rather than float.

In the short years of my youth, the environment ethic of our culture began a transformation. By the time I was a teenager, it was no longer acceptable to throw trash out of the car window. We began to admire those whose behavior protected and nurtured the world around us, and to eschew those whose behavior was destructive to the world around us. It wasn't a complete transformation, and some areas changed more quickly than others.

Hitchhiking in Georgia back in the mid-seventies, when this transformation was well underway in most of the country, I glimpsed a corner of the culture that wasn't ready to change yet. My friend Scott Stuckey and I caught a ride with the perfect stereotype of the southern redneck. After several miles, he threw his empty beer bottle out his window to crash on the pavement. He must have seen the surprise on our faces, because he commented about "giving those government leeches something to do."

That image has always hung with me. It's one of those moments that just doesn't fit well into the way I see the world. Considering the rest of what came out of the guy's mouth, you'd think he loved the place where he lived. Yet, he felt perfectly justified in damaging the wonder he said he liked, and he justified it in his mind with the assumption that someone should be coming along behind him to clean up his mess.

I recall that long-ago incident as I negotiate around the glass and debris, wondering how we get to the point where it's okay in our mind to leave a mess for someone else to clean up. Maybe we all do it in our own little ways, and some are more destructive than others. From the coworker who leaves her dirty dishes in the common kitchen sink all day, to big oil companies who destroy entire ecosystems, are we all guilty of some level of transgression?

I suppose big cultural transformations take time.

•

Treat the earth well, it was not given to you by your parents, it was loaned to you by your children.

Native American proverb (Also one translation of "Hozho")

•

Tuba City is a little Navaho town in northern Arizona, right at the edge of the Hopi Tribe. Dave and I pull up to the Moenkopi Legacy Inn, and check in to an excellent room. We easily settle in to the routine we developed last summer when we toured together: unpacking, showering, doing laundry in the sink, hanging clothes to dry, and walking to a relaxing supper.

Ahhhh. The comfort of a familiar routine out in the desert of unfamiliar exploration. Dark chocolate for the soul.

19

DESERT SCOOTERS

Time isn't used, it's experienced.

Hopi proverb

DAY 12 • TUBA CITY TO KAYENTA, ARIZONA

An easy 75 mile day in front of us lets us enjoy a leisurely breakfast at Denny's. Unless the wind is hard on us, we should get done in less than eight hours. After a relaxing breakfast, we meet some interesting folks as we're headed toward the door. A small group of five—two couples plus an extra friend. They've got a truck with a trailer, and the trailer holds a couple little Vespa-type scooters. The gals ride the scooters along the highway, and the fellas follow along in the truck. When the gals get tired of "scooting," the guys pick them up and trailer the scooters. It's a grand adventure for them. They've always wanted to take a trip like this along the highways of the Southwest. When they hit the high plains of Texas in a few days, they'll just ride in the truck to avoid the heat.

I'm curious about why they choose the little scooters. Why not motorcycles? They could all ride that way, and experience the road together. They say it's because the scooters are so much more fuel-efficient. I'm sure a quizzical look crosses my face as I do some quick mental math on the combined fuel efficiency of the big truck with a trailer *plus* the two scooters. I'm having a hard time making the math work.

As they continue talking, I arrive at the heart of the story: Scooters are way more cute. Cute matters, as I've learned from my daughter.

The conversation gives me a good deal to think about as Dave and I pedal east along US 160 into a sun that's already risen. On the one hand, it's neat that the scooter group decided to take this trip in a way that gets a couple of them out of the steel and glass capsule, and into the wind and grit to experience the trail. It's admirable that the two gals are bent on getting more of the "real experience." I'm riding my bicycle across the country for similar reasons.

Yet, there's a part of me that wants to be critical of them. As soon as the road gets hot, they have the truck pick them up. Sounds like they only ride about three hours a day. And the whole Texas thing about riding in the truck the whole time really bothers me: I'd dearly *love* to put together a bicycle trip across the legendary Staked Plains of West Texas someday, to experience that place more like the great Comanches who ruled over the area for hundreds of years. Yet these folks are gonna pack up their scooters and ride in the air conditioning at high speed across it.

Why's it so easy to fall into the sort of elitist criticism that I'm allowing to run through my mind this morning? Because I'm riding a bicycle and carrying everything myself, without a vehicle following to pick me up? Does this make me and my trip more *valid* than the trip the scooter folks are taking? If I wanted real *validity* on the trip, I'd walk barefoot and live on grasshoppers and beetles. There's a commonality I should be celebrating, rather than picking apart the differences. The scooter gals had an idea really similar to the idea Dave and I had, we're just implementing the ideas differently. I should find the harmony between our ideas, rather than the dissonance.

•

Hozho. It's a Navajo word that translates roughly into the beauty found in the perfect balance and harmony people should pursue and maintain in life. I focus my mind on celebrating my commonality with these scooter folks, and the morning light takes on a new and better hue.

Dave and I pass an RV pulled off the road, apparently having spent the night there on the shoulder. As we roll past, we hear conversation in the RV, and smell bacon cooking. It's been an hour or so since breakfast, and the bacon smells mighty fine. In fact, the smell and the glimpse of conversation as we pass make me feel mighty *Hozho-y.*

We stop and fill water bottles and take in a few calories in Tonalea before continuing down the road. About fifteen miles east of Tonalea, I stop to fix a flat, something I'm surprised I'm not getting more of with all the debris on the side of the road. When I catch up with Dave, he's leaning on his bike, chatting with Lawrence, who operates the BBQ stand on the side of the road. As I approach, I find myself looking around, wondering how a guy can make a living out of a BBQ stand out here in the middle of the desert.

Dave and I are both a bit too hot to want BBQ, but we enjoy chatting with Lawrence. We learn way more about his health issues than we really want to know, and it's clear that Lawrence would like us to hang out and chat some more. Dave and I both feel bad when we let him know we've got to be pushing on east if we're gonna make it to Kayenta.

I love these short days. They give us the time to stop and chat with guys like Lawrence. A day where I cover a lot of miles gives me a good sense of accomplishment, and is nice sometimes, but an easy day with lots of time of lollygagging is a real joy.

Hozho.

•

Wisdom comes only when you stop looking for it and start living the life the Creator intended for you.

Hopi proverb

•

While it's hot today, it's not dangerously hot. The high pushes close to 100, but doesn't cross that century line. A few miles further up the road we come to another convenience store where we can fill bottles and gather food. There's shade out front, and Dave and I lean against the cool concrete block wall in that shade, enjoying food and drink.

We're sharing the shade with a group of dogs. They're keeping their distance, but watching us closely in case we drop any snacks. The ubiquitous res dogs along the road here have a consistent look, probably some herding dog roots with a lot of other stuff mixed in. We stop eating while we still have a few scraps left, sharing with our new canine friends.

Finishing our day in Kayenta late in the afternoon, we're feeling plenty of *Hozho*. We've had a tailwind nearly all day long, and while there's been some rough and crappy pavement, far more of the miles we rode today were on smooth pavement.

•

The Best Western Wetherill Inn is just a mile north of Highway 160, and they let us check in early. Next door to the motel is a great little diner where they serve a chicken-fried steak that's truly a work of art. Nothing says *Hozho* like a slab of chicken-fried steak cooked in a cast iron skillet with lots of grease, balanced superbly with mashed potatoes, and brought into divine harmony with perfect gravy.

20

HOZHO

*Take a breath of the new dawn
and make it a part of you.*

Hopi proverb

DAY 13 • KAYENTA, ARIZONA TO TOWAOC, COLORADO

The first hints of bloom are creeping into the eastern sky as we pedal east out of Kayenta in the morning. A warm blush washes across the desert around us, revealing stunning beauty, seeping into my heart and soul, pushing strength and energy into my body.

The mountains and rocks here have been washed by oceans and chiseled by winds over the eons. As dawn along the horizon spreads brilliant red across the eastern sky, the red sand and rock around us is transformed into a deep red mystical world punctuated by the quiet of the empty road. I can't imagine a human looking across this desert in this light and not thinking of it as sacred.

How many places on earth can offer a sunrise this stunning? Riding east into the rising sun, floating through the desert lavishness around me, my legs fill with endless energy. I keep slowing myself down, knowing that we've got over 100 miles to ride today. The magic of this place percolates into my body and soul, wrapping me in a spiritual high. The line between physical and spiritual blurs: the physical rising and falling with the spiritual like a small boat on a tide, the spiritual breathing life into the physical. When the breath of the spiritual subsides, the strength and vigor of the physical wanes.

Hozho.

I feel like a racehorse crashing out of the gates, bent on gulping every moment the world has in front of me right now.

Life is good.

At about 45 miles, we come to a little place called Mexican Water and I do some gulping of a different sort—about half a gallon of vanilla milkshake. This is our breakfast stop, but as it often the case, we end up eating cheeseburgers for breakfast. A milkshake on top of a greasy cheeseburger is a fantastic idea, right? A big rich milkshake that'll sit and curdle in my stomach for the next few hours as we make our way across a hot desert . . .

Stated that way, I know it doesn't sound like such a great idea. But sitting in an air-conditioned diner, enjoying the coolness and wanting more of it, an icy milkshake sounds really wonderful. Intellectually, I know what's going to happen. I know this won't turn out well. But I do it anyway.

Why the heck do we do this to ourselves? Are we pre-wired for self destructive behavior? I can't even begin to count instances in my life when I've watched smart and sane people dive headlong into a night of drunken debauchery fully aware of the high price they'll pay the next day. Or folks who maintain high calorie intake diets day after day, knowing full well that they're saturating themselves with weight and goop that will significantly deteriorate their quality of life all the way up to the point that it kills them early.

I'm sure psychologists have all sorts of "reasons" for this behavior. There must be a few folks who are immune to it, but it's a pretty small percentage in the culture I've observed, and certainly doesn't include me. Is it an internal collective lemming-type behavior, truly trying to bring about self-destruction? Maybe some sort of psychological pathology bred into us by a common ancestor way back in time who just happened to have some other traits that evolution selected for, and we just got this dark tendency by accident?

Maybe it *is* lemming-like. If so, I just took a huge leap off the vanilla milkshake and cheeseburger cliff, and I pay a heavy price as I push my mushy legs around the pedals headed east out of Mexican Water. That cheeseburger grease and heavy cream curdles nicely in my gut, urged on by a broiling sun baking down on me.

This self-induced gastronomical hurt-locker stretches out in front of me for a lot of miles, so I settle down into a miserable pity-party, and watch Dave hurtle on up the road without me. Wallowing in my suffering, I imagine that wind could have a big impact on me right now. A friendly tailwind would drown my bellyache in the pleasure of the ride, while a bad wind would dig this black hole of misery deeper.

With that thought, I cast a jinx. A nasty crosswind pushes against my right shoulder. Just as the euphoria I felt this morning boosted my physical well-being, my current milkshake misery pummels my tolerance for the wind that's blowing in my ears. Dave seems unfazed by either the milkshake or the crosswind, cranking away at his steady pace. Mr. Consistency.

Misery, like the Sirens of the ancient Greeks, lulls our mind into numb acceptance, and we fall deeper and deeper into the hole of loathing, unable to see joy around us. I know this is happening to me as I force my legs to turn the pedals, and I struggle to find a mast onto which I can lash myself to avoid falling into a pit of despair. I remember the wonderful euphoria I was feeling all morning *before* breakfast, and try to keep my focus on the goodness the memory brings. I begin to enjoy the ever-evolving desert beauty around me again.

We pick up water and snacks at Red Mesa, about 13 miles

down the road. Dave and I both find ourselves pretty self-conscious about how *different* we are from those around us. There's a certain amount of difference that comes with riding a bicycle down the highway anyhow—dressed in spandex and cycling gear as we are—but the difference runs deeper than spandex today.

We're white. Nobody else is.

We're the only non-Indian folks at the combination grocery/gas station where we're gathering food and drink. I imagine it's a bit uncommon for white folks to ever stop here—a little hole in the wall place in a little hole in the wall town in the middle of the dry and dusty high desert. White folks who are wearing wild cycling gear steps it up yet another notch on the "different" scale.

Not that I feel worried or threatened; quite the opposite. *I'm* acutely aware of my difference, but feel like everyone around me is politely trying *not* to see that difference. This might be part of the Navajo culture: respect for the privacy and *self* of someone else. If a Navajo walked into a swank all-white suburban cappuccino bar, I doubt he'd get this same respect.

Eighteen miles down the road we come to a crossroad where US 160 takes a left, putting the wind at our back. The milkshake abuse I heaped on my gut a couple hours ago has had time to heal, and we pull into another of the combination grocery/gas stations for more water and calories.

I hesitate to call these places we've been stopping at as we've crossed the reservation *convenience stores*. Like so many we've stopped at, this one was a full-fledged grocery store, albeit small. There's no branding from a national chain, and feels like a family run business. It seems to be a place where local folks gather everything they need from a grocery, and spend a few extra minutes socializing with other patrons. Truly a "general store."

I'm fascinated by a corner packed with bundles of herbs, all sorts of different medicinal herbs that you'd be hard-pressed to find elsewhere, desert plants and sage and that sort of thing. I wonder how much of this stuff is sold to folks who live around here, who use it in their daily life, and how much of it is for the benefit of touristy folks like us. Judging from the dearth of touristy folks, and the wealth of local folks, I have to imagine at least some of it's used locally.

There's not a standard soda machine, with ice for my water bottles. I ask the guy at the counter if he has any ice, and he tells me to walk into the back and take whatever we want. "The back" is mostly the butcher counter, and the fella back there is cutting meat. He points me to a big bucket in the corner where there's ice, and I grab enough to fill my bottles. I thank him, and he gives me a nod and one of the most heart-felt smiles I've ever received.

Sitting outside in the shade of the front porch, I'm a bit ashamed of the satisfaction I take in sensing that Dave is as worn-out as I am. I was beginning to think he'd taken on su-perhero qualities with his steady pace in that nasty crosswind. Sharing a sleeve of Fig Newtons, we talk about how unusual it feels for us to be the "different ones." As a white middle-class male, it's been rare in my life when I've stuck out as "the different one."

A glorious tailwind pushes us across the last 30-something miles for the day. We pass Four Corners Monument scream-ing down a wonderful descent, cross a river, and start a gentle uphill grade that will last the rest of the day. Even a gentle uphill grade is a delight when there's a wind at my back. In fact, I think a gentle uphill grade with a tailwind might be my favorite riding condition. I get to find a nice steady rhythm in the pedals, which falls into harmony with a good healthy heart rate. I feel like I'm putting in a healthy workload, and get to enjoy the beauty around me. My head's up, the scent of the desert is pouring through my nostrils, the sounds around me are sweet. I'm making solid progress across the pavement.

Life is good.

Hozho.

Mr. Consistency seems as unaffected by this glorious

tailwind as he was by the evil crosswind. I'm off and running down the road with the wind at my back, while Dave clicks along at what seems the exact pace he sets no matter what's happening around him.

It's not that Dave is taking it easy with the tailwind; he's working hard and ready for the day to be over. While I'd been there in that exact place a few miles back when the wind was messing with me, I'm now feeling great and would be happy to ride another 50 miles today with this great tailwind. While the tailwind pours new life into me, it's doing nothing at all for Dave.

The effect wind has on me is more mental than physical. From a physical perspective, I should be able to set my gears so I'm putting out the physical effort I want to put out, and go whatever speed that gives me. When I'm fighting the wind, it's a slower speed; when the wind is helping me, it's a faster speed. It shouldn't be that big a deal.

But it is.

Somewhere deep down inside, I feel cheated by a headwind. I feel I'm not making the forward progress I should be making for the effort I'm putting in. On top of this, the constant gale screaming in my ears irritates me, making it difficult to find the joy in the ride.

A tailwind, on the other hand, is one of the most beautiful experiences you can have on a bike. There's no wind in my ears, so I hear everything around me. The chain purrs sweetly as it pulls the gears under the coaxing of my legs. The soft hiss of my tires on the smooth hard pavement, the sound of little critters scurrying in the desert around me as I pass. Smells aren't as big a deal out here in the dry desert, but even the smells are more accessible in a tailwind, since I'm moving through air at a slower relative speed, and the smells linger around my face long enough to register and enjoy them.

Relative progress, speed, sights, smells, sounds. It all goes together to create a gestalt for the ride that's pure sweetness, and I never want it to end.

Hozho.

After gliding through 30 miles of this sweet gestalt, we roll into a big casino in the little town of Towaoc in Colorado. Dave and I take advantage of an inexpensive room that's pretty darned nice. We pay something like $50 for the room for the night. I'm sure the rates are much higher on weekends, but it's a Sunday night, and the laws of supply and demand work in our favor. (Or is it Monday night?. . .)

We wander through the casino to get to supper, then back to the room. Casino designers are smart that way, leading patrons past gaming tables and machines at every opportunity, dangling enticement with every step.

There's not much here that tempts me though. I look for folks who appear to be having fun, but can't find any. Row after row of sad faces hooked up to slot machines like arms connected to IV's, drugs pumping into their minds. Table after table of drained souls looking to leave scraps of happiness and dignity on the green felt of the blackjack table.

I'm sure happiness finds its way into the hearts and minds of the folks here sometimes, but none of it shows on their faces today. In fact, I've rarely seen it on any of the forays I've made into gambling cathedrals during my life.

In a casino, it feels like everyone's working against a headwind. The constant clang of the slots is the pounding of the wind in their ears. But just out of reach is the promise of a tailwind, so they keep pedaling in misery, hoping for that little wind at their back soon. At tightly prescribed intervals, the road turns for a short distance, and they feel that sweet wind on their back.

Just for a little bit. The game is carefully rigged to make sure the road turns back into the wind quickly after meting out a tiny dose of "feel-good." It doesn't take much to keep the hopeful soul hooked up to the misery. Those little periods of tailwind are sweet enough to keep the gambler throwing his money down the pit, hoping for that next turn.

The unsmiling faces I see in the casino reflect a deep

sadness to me. Perhaps a sense that no matter how hard they pedal, they're still sliding backwards. The occasional burst of tailwind pumps just enough joy drug into their veins to keep them pedaling for a while longer . . .

But then, maybe I'm projecting something inside myself onto the sad faces I see around me. In fairness, I have to say I have many friends who say they truly enjoy going to casinos to gamble. I don't mean to judge folks who enjoy it, or folks like me who don't. I'm just observing, and it's something I just don't understand. Nobody forces these people to come to the casino. They know they're most likely going to walk out the door with less money than they walked in with. And while they're here, I'm just not seeing many smiles.

Then again, who am I to talk about silly behavior after my milkshake debacle at breakfast?

COLORAAADO

21

ELEVATING

Earth teach me quiet ~ as the grasses are still with new light.
Earth teach me suffering ~ as old stones suffer with memory.
Earth teach me humility ~ as blossoms are humble with be-
ginning.
Earth teach me caring ~ as mothers nurture their young.
Earth teach me courage ~ as the tree that stands alone.
Earth teach me limitation ~ as the ant that crawls on the
ground.
Earth teach me freedom ~ as the eagle that soars in the sky.
Earth teach me acceptance ~ as the leaves that die each fall.
Earth teach me renewal ~ as the seed that rises in the spring.
Earth teach me to forget myself ~ as melted snow forgets
its life.
Earth teach me to remember kindness ~ as dry fields weep
with rain.

A Ute prayer

DAY 13 • TOWAOC TO DURANGO, COLORADO

Mounting up in early light and cool morning air, we begin our
day riding through wisps of fog now and again, something I
haven't seen since I left the Pacific coast. The moisture in the

air feels delicious as it hydrates the membranes of my lungs and sinuses.

Colorado isn't a place known for moist air. When folks come out to visit us in Colorado, they usually complain about how dry the air is. But this morning, as I begin to climb back into my home state, I'm struck by how much more humid it is than the desert air I've been riding through for the last couple weeks.

There's active irrigation along the highway, so lush green fields spill welcome moist air down on us as we ride. Big commercial sprinklers pour water across the green fields, sparkling like fountains of gems in the early morning light. The peaks of the Rockies in the distance grow closer with each mile. It feels like home, and it feels good.

A cyclist's perspective on the wildlife in an area is often a reflection of the dead stuff we see smashed on the road as we roll past it. This morning, the roadkill reflects a big change in habitat: a possum and raccoon, a snake now and again. The moist environment created by the irrigation supports a whole new community of critters.

We roll into Cortez after about 12 miles. We'd like to get another 10 or 15 miles in before breakfast, but figure this is our best shot. We pull into a little diner, and strike up a conversation with a guy out front. He tells us the road over to Durango is mostly downhill, except the uphill parts. A comedian. Taking on a serious expression, he amends his description to, "You go up for a while, then it's all downhill." I'm still not sure what to think, but realize I'm better off not asking, as his comments have now set expectations inside me.

Expectations: sometimes a dangerous thing. This morning, eating our breakfast at a Cortez diner, I'm building a complete picture in my mind of what the rest of the day is supposed to be. Predictably, I'm disappointed when reality doesn't meet my expectation.

I really don't think this is a particularly tough stretch of road. Sure there's quite a bit of uphill once you head east out of Cortez, but we are, after all, in the Rocky Mountains. More than anything, I think the problem I've created for myself is that I decided at breakfast that it was going to be an "easy" day since it was only 60 miles or so with about the same amount of climbing we had yesterday.

I'm rolling along, holding a steady pace up a long climb, when movement catches my eye off to the right. In a small tree about 20 yards off the road, a Golden Eagle pushes big buckets of air down under his wings, climbs thirty feet, and glides off across a meadow. He's a beautiful creature, and at this close range, his size is breathtaking.

We eventually find that downhill section, and roll down a long and wonderful descent into Durango. Our riding time today was only four and a half hours, and our total elapsed time for the day was just a little over six hours.

With such a short day, we take the afternoon to do laundry, eat a big dinner, and drink a couple beers. For the next few days, our mileage is going to stay relatively short, and we're looking forward to some wonderful mountain scenery.

22

DEEP BLUE MOUNTAIN SKIES

It is by riding a bicycle that you learn the contours of a country best, since you have to sweat up the hills and coast down them. Thus you remember them as they actually are, while in a motor car only a high hill impresses you, and you have no such accurate remembrance of country you have driven through as you gain by riding a bicycle.

Ernest Hemingway

DAY 14 • DURANGO TO PAGOSA SPRINGS, COLORADO

Durango is a big bicycle town. Some world-class cyclists hail from these parts, and many times I've heard of the great road cycling in the area. In addition, there's a strong road cycling club here, and Ft. Lewis College in Durango has what they bill as the "#1 cycling program in the nation," with 17 national championships. There's a really fun ride I occasionally do down here over the Memorial Day weekend, called the Iron Horse Classic. It's a ride/race from Durango to Silverton, racing the old steam engine up into the mountains. Lots of climbing, about 50 miles, and they close the road for a couple hours for the race.

All this helped to color my expectations for the day. I'm

imagining that cars in the area are accustomed to cyclists, and that the roads will accommodate safe riding. Once again, my expectations set me up for disappointment.

Riding east on US 160 out of Durango is one of the most treacherous sections of highway I've encountered on my ride thus far. There's no shoulder, and the traffic early in the morning is extremely heavy. The first few miles are fine, as the highway is divided, but as soon at the highway narrows down to two lanes, it's terror. Generally speaking, Colorado motorists are better than the average U.S. driver when it comes to accepting cyclists on the road, but with the morning volume and narrow road, there's just no way this can be a safe ride.

Crossing Arizona, I was generally impressed with the highways I rode on. There was almost always a shoulder appropriate to the traffic. I've arrived at my home state in a town that's one of the cycling capitals of the nation, and am enduring some of the most dangerous riding I've faced. The good news is that after 10 or 15 miles, the highway grows a bit of a shoulder, and the traffic thins out. By the time Dave and I hit Bayfield, there's a decent shoulder. By Piedra, it's actually a pleasant ride.

We stop at a little truck farm with a general store in Piedra for some calories. They've just planted their vegetables in what appears to be a five acre garden, and a big commercial impact rotor throws a mighty arc of water across the newly planted garden with a slow and steady rhythm. It's a mighty short growing season here in the mountains, and I can't imagine that a person can raise enough on these few acres to make a go of it. Sitting in the shade out on the deck, I wonder if the general store can possibly turn enough profit to support a garden operation that might break even at best. But I can't imagine this either, out here in the middle of nowhere, and in the 30 minutes we spend here, no other customers walk in the door. There must have been some capital that helped these folks buy this property and the store, and maybe enough cash flow to finance keeping the store stocked and the garden planted.

But can they possibly turn a profit year to year? I suppose it's possible, but my common-sense business logic can't fathom how, let alone how they can pull any sort of living income from the operation.

What is it that drives folks to take on these sorts of operations? Sometimes when people get laid off, they try their hand at making a go of some sort of self-employment. In most cases, the results are far less glamorous and supportable than they envisioned. The work is usually harder than expected, the hours longer than desired, and the income less than hoped-for. In many cases, folks spend their life savings to make a go of some dream enterprise, only to lose the whole kit'n'kaboodle. Of course, there are some success stories as well, but I suspect these success stories are far outweighed by the stories of failures that don't get told.

Yet, year after year, folks dive into these commercial dreams with zeal, often displaying far more optimism than common sense. Even so, chatting with the middle-aged woman who runs the store, I have zero doubt that she's as happy as she's ever been in her life. She exudes goodwill and joy. While I don't get to chat with the old fellow in the garden who's presumably her husband, he has a way and a walk about him that shouts *contentment*. He sits in the shade for a spell, then hops on his little ATV and motors out to one of the irrigation heads, and moves it to a new place or a new angle. Then back to the shade to watch water cascade across his garden to the soft and steady rhythm of the sprinkler heads.

Who knows, maybe they do make an economic go of it. I have no idea what the real story is. I've just fabricated this whole scenario in my mind based on a couple of clues. Who am I to say? I doubt I'd loan money to an enterprise like this, but I sure admire the hope these folks clearly have in their hearts, and the happiness and joy I see in their life.

It's perfect weather for cycling today. Warm but not hot, somewhere in the 80s, with the morning low for the day a little under 50 degrees. Dave and I stay warm all day, but never uncomfortably hot. The highway winds its way through a patchwork of roadside wildflowers, bordered by pine forest climbing above on one side and falling away on the other. A crystal clear Colorado sky opens above us, a blue so deep it makes you dizzy. The occasional bright white wispy cloud dances across the firmament, punctuating the deep blue vault of heaven stretching over this paradise.

We've reached Colorado elevation now, and we're staying here for a few days. It feels like home to me. It's not really the landscape around me, because where I live on the Eastern Slope of the Rockies, it's more high desert than the mountain pine we're riding through today. It's the elevation that's making me feel a bit "at home."

Usually, when we think of "home," we're thinking in two dimensions, a place on a flat map. I'm realizing that riding at 5,000 and 6,000 feet and above feels like "home" elevation to me. I live at 6000 feet, and I do most of my riding at elevations like that.

Back in Twentynine Palms on my first rest day, the book I picked up at the musty, used bookstore was a short little novel about a Ute family that lived in *this* area of Colorado around the year 1900. When I picked the book up, I didn't realize it was set *here*, but now that I'm here, I'm remembering clearly the descriptions of Pagosa, Piedra, and other nearby places here in southwest Colorado. In my mind, I relive little bits of the novel as I ride through the landscape.

Coincidence. I'm often struck by the frequency of "coincidences" like this. Of all the books I might pick up at that little used bookstore in the California desert, what are the odds that I'd pick one up that's set in a place I'll be riding right through? Life leaves little breadcrumbs along the path for us to find. Sometimes we get too busy making our way down the path to notice the breadcrumbs, or pick them up when we see them, or think much about them if we do pick them up.

The older I get, the better I am at noticing more along the path, and picking stuff up. Even when it doesn't seem to mean much, I often wonder if the tiny breadcrumbs help us navigate our way down paths the universe needs us to take. They might seem small at first glance, but often a small change in trajectory translates to big differences in life down the road. Like an arrow shot from a bow. A tiny change in trajectory at the point the arrow leaves the bowstring becomes a larger and larger change the further the arrow travels from the bowstring. Where we travel and land in life is generally determined by tiny changes in trajectory that happened way back down the path we've been on.

23

COWBOY UP

*True merit, like a river, the deeper it is,
the less noise it makes.*

Edward Frederick Halifax

DAY 15 • PAGOSA SPRINGS TO ALAMOSA, COLORADO

Saddled up and pedaling in the pre-dawn moisture-laden air, we meander through sleepy Pagosa Springs toward a bright mountain sunrise. We stop on the east side of town to calorie up a bit. Scarfing something down that's loaded with calories but probably terribly unhealthy, I watch a couple cowboys fuel up their truck and come in to pay.

Of course, I don't know how much real cowboyin' these fellas do, but they're dressed the part, with spurs and the whole shebang. They're not the first cowboy types we've seen along US 160 through southern Colorado, and I find myself wondering about how much the fancy duds are to help the fellas show off and play a part, and how much they really add to the practicality of their day.

I've met a couple real cowboys in my life, and I've seen an awful lot of fellas who like to dress the part without any real need. Drugstore cowboys we used to call them. The real ones tend to be a lot less flash and sparkle, and tend to carry themselves with a lot more humility. I suppose the real work that cowboyin' involves helps a fella grow accustomed to the taste of humble pie.

Many years ago, as a young idealist just out of college and pretty sure I knew most of the important stuff, I met an old guy down in southern Arizona who helped me along toward understanding just how little I really knew. His name was Archie, and he was probably one of the last real cowboys around. This was in the mid seventies, and he was probably ninety-plus at the time, so I imagine he was born in the 1870s.

Archie's home was an old broken-down trailer deep in the southern Arizona desert. I spent a couple weeks camped a couple miles from his trailer, and spent a good deal of time with him, listening to him, learning from him. We'd sit around a campfire in the evening, and Archie would spin yarns about his days working horses and cattle across the Southwest. It was a desolate, hard, dangerous life he'd survived, and his tales often included fellas who weren't as lucky at the survival sweepstakes as he was. By the time he was 20, he'd learned more about physical pain and discomfort than most folks learn in a lifetime. He became a solitary and self-sufficient man, who wandered from job to job as the wanderlust tickled his fancy. A seeker of adventure far more than a seeker of fortune, Archie had several stories of small fortunes gained and squandered.

Before I met Archie, my stereotype of a cowboy was that of an arrogant and insecure dandy. Archie couldn't have been further from that. He was soft-spoken, an aura of self-confidence wrapped around everything he did. He didn't wear spurs that jangled as he walked, choosing instead to let his soft-spoken self-assurance speak with every step. He didn't wear tight jeans and shiny shirts; instead, letting the tattered and work-ragged jackets and pants speak of hard work and well-earned calluses.

We've created quite a mythology around the cowboy, and an awful lot of folks in our culture today like to emulate and worship that mythology. In reality, these guys were probably mostly misfits with an overdeveloped wanderlust and outsized sense of adventure. Most of them dabbled a bit on whichever side of the law was convenient at any given time, always looking for the path most heavily laced with adrenaline.

On the one hand, I find it easy to be quietly critical of the guys today who dress the part of the mythological cowboy. While many or most of them might be honest and hard-working folks, I can't help but feel that they're chasing a myth, not the real cowboy. On the other hand, I realize that for the most part, a *real* cowboy living in today's world would never survive. They'd end up in jail at an early age, and become institutional criminals.

Is there enough adventure in our world today to support the real cowboy? Can we suffer enough and endure enough discomfort to condition ourselves to the life they lived? I listen to the spurs jingling on the boots of the fella walking back to his truck after paying with a credit card. I suspect he's a hard-workin' fella. But would he fit Archie's definition of a cowboy? I notice as he gets into his truck that his windows are rolled up. The AC in his shiny truck must work just fine.

Here I am dressed in spandex and a bright jersey, with a nice GPS mounted on my handlebars to tell me where I am. I regale myself in the myth and garb of the cyclist in the same way the fella with the spurs regales himself in the myth and garb of the cowboy. We all wrap ourselves in the mythology we want other people to see us in.

I look east at the mountains ahead of us, and figure I've got a bit of sufferin' in my near future this morning.

24

WOLF CREEK PASS

We are now in the mountains and they are in us, kindling enthusiasm, making every nerve quiver, filling every pore and cell of us.

John Muir, *My First Summer in the Sierra*

HAPPY BIRTHDAY

The broadly winding road sweeps us steadily up toward the Continental Divide as I apply steady pressure to the pedals headed east out of Pagosa. Bright morning sunlight breaks over the peaks in front of us, slanting down onto the lush meadows rolling past us. Light traffic is a bonus on this beautiful morning.

The grade kicks up, signaling the beginning of several miles of climbing at 7 and 8 percent. I feel like I've finally come into decent riding shape after making it this far across the country, wondering if I'll be able to keep up with Dave on this climb, so kick my output up slightly and pull around Dave at the base of the climb.

Dave is nearly always stronger than I am. Every now and then, he'll have a bad day when I'm having a good day, and I'll be able to ride harder than he does, but it's rare. I wonder if I might have a slight advantage since I have close to a thousand more miles under my belt on this trip than he does. Unfortunately, soon after we start the steep climb, a really nice view up a tumbling creek opens up on our right, and I pull over to take a picture. When I finish up and start putting pressure on the pedals again, Dave is a hundred yards up the road. From here to the top of the pass, I watch the familiar site of Dave's back as he pulls further and further away up the road ahead of me.

The climb is wonderful, with good road, light traffic, and a wide shoulder. The steady grade makes it easy to find a gear that works, and just crank. It's the kind of climbing that lets me find that perfect sweet spot where heart rate, respiration, pedal cadence, and perspiration seem in perfect tune and harmony.

Nearing the top of the climb, I realize it's my birthday today. I'm 57 years old as I top the pass and pull off to chat and take a couple pictures with Dave. I can't imagine very many ways to spend a birthday that would be more gratifying than the climb I just did.

Flying down the east side of Wolf Creek Pass on pavement that's glassy smooth, I touch the brakes twice from the top all the way to the bottom. I'm pulled through long sweeping curves, leaning hard into the corners. I'm certain wisdom would slow me down a little bit, but my thirst for the joy of falling down the sweep of the road as fast as I can casts wisdom over my shoulder as I cascade down the smooth descent.

The drop buffers down into a gentle downhill grade. A tailwind has developed for us, and we glide down the highway from the base of Wolf Creek Pass at a screaming pace, before stopping for an early lunch at South Fork.

Leaving South Fork, we enjoy four or five miles of quartering tailwind, painting a smile on my face. My smile begins to fade as I feel the wind shifting, and in a matter of ten minutes, it's made its way 180 degrees around the compass, and has begun slapping me in the face. The smile has faded. I'm suffering. I'm pissed.

Dave pulls around me, and steadily fades away up the

road from me as I slog through the miserable miles. He just puts his head down and pedals. He's able to make himself oblivious to the joy-robbing wind pounding against his face. Mr. Consistency.

Dave sometimes wonders if I find more joy in life than he does. He's not saying that my life has more joy in it, but just that I seem more able to notice and savor the joy that's there. I don't really know if he's right or not, but if he is, then it's also true that Dave notices adversity less than I do. He just takes the wind shift in stride. He gears down and just keeps pedaling. If it's true that I can exploit a moment of joy for all it's worth, then it's equally true that I'm more fully trounced and demoralized by a moment of misery.

The wind pushes against our faces all the way to Monte Vista. By the time we stop at a convenience store there, I've got my misery tolerance dialed in, and am okay with the upcoming 20 miles into the wind to close out the day.

It's beautiful and magical what a difference this makes for me. I don't know if the wind really dies back a bit, or if my acceptance of it just makes it tolerable. Whatever the reason, the final 20 miles of the day into Alamosa is pretty darned pleasant.

Like Durango, Alamosa is a college town. Not a big university city like Boulder, Colorado or Columbus, Ohio, but a small town with a small college. I like these towns a lot, and Dave and I find a quirky bar/eatery downtown, where we enjoy supper and a beer. We rode 96 miles today, with a great climb and a joyful descent. The wind was behind us for a while, and ahead of us for a while, and I found a way to make peace with the headwind by the time the day ended. We averaged 13.6 miles per hour and get to spend the evening in a great little college town. Life is good.

This is the last night out on this leg of our journey across the U.S. We celebrate with a beer as we enjoy supper. Well, maybe two beers.

25

FLYING WITH THE WIND

*I ride because I am addicted to the endorphins and to the
adrenaline. I ride because the second my legs start turning
circles I become a happier person. I ride because I love to
feel the wind on my face and listen to the birds and bugs.
I ride because it allows me to take out my aggression and
anger. I ride because it stabilizes my life and creates balance.
I ride because going downhill at 40 miles per hour makes
me feel free. I ride because I can't cry and pedal and the
same time. I ride because it allows me to play with the boys.
I ride because I can go alone. I ride because even though
I have ridden the route 1000 times, I never know what is
around the next bend.*

Emily Kachorek

DAY 16 • ALAMOSA TO WALSENBURG, COLORADO

Leaving Alamosa in the pale morning light, we roll into another beautiful Rocky Mountain morning. Damp air hangs close
to the ground in places, almost a light fog. Today we'll ride
to Walsenburg, where this leg of the journey will pause. The
next leg will take us out into Kansas. The sadness I feel on this
last day of riding for this leg of our journey across the U.S. is

more than I expected. I find myself holding back and riding a bit slow, savoring the last morsels of the journey.

Dave, on the other hand, has what he calls "headed back to the barn" syndrome. Dave grew up on a farm, and has some wonderfully quirky sayings like this. For those who have no idea what "headed back to the barn" means, it refers to how horses behave when you've had them out working and they realize they're headed home, or how dairy cows behave when they're headed for the barn at milking time.

I don't think Dave necessarily wants the trip to end. He's been enjoying himself as much as I have. The difference is the checkmark. Reaching our end-point means Dave gets to put a checkmark beside this accomplishment. He's completed an important milestone. This gives him great pleasure.

I want to check that box on my list too, but I'm not as driven by it as Dave is. I'm guessing that for Dave, he's finding growing joy as he nears the end-point where he'll put that big fat "x" in the box beside this section of the ride. For me, the day is bittersweet as each pedal stroke brings me closer to the end of the joy I've been experiencing for the past three weeks.

Dave has to stop and wait for me several times during the morning. He's good-natured about it as always, but I can sense the giddy-up in him as he draws closer to that barn with each mile. My giddy-up is broken this morning.

We hope to find a breakfast place at either Blanca or Ft. Garland, but end up settling for convenience store food at Ft. Garland. It's our last convenience store meal, and as silly as it sounds, I think I'll miss these meals, sitting around on the shady concrete in front of the store, people watching while we eat and drink.

Leaving Ft. Garland, we pick up a little tailwind. On any other day, this would lift my spirits so high that I'd be flying out in front of Dave, sucking up the joy of screaming along the highway in front of the wind. Today, the joy of the tailwind is lost on me. I look for every opportunity to take it easy and savor every morsel of these last miles.

Approaching La Veta pass, I notice a small herd of elk grazing in a meadow down to the right. I stop to take a picture, but when I stop, they head into the woods. When I catch up to Dave at the top of the pass, I ask if he saw the elk, and he's bummed that he didn't. At this point, Dave is so focused on that checkmark at the end of the ride that he's seeing very little around him, while I'm so focused on what's around me that I'm probably frustrating Dave with my lollygagging.

I decide to let go of the stalling, and just go with the wind between here and Walsenburg where we'll end the day. Flying down the mountain with a tailwind, I think one car passes me the whole time. It's a long and gradual descent, and I don't think I touch the brakes once. As the grade levels out, I pass a smear on the pavement where a big cow elk was hit overnight, the smear ending at a big pile of cow elk off on the side of the road. I smile to myself as I figure I'll tease Dave about how he couldn't possibly have missed *this* elk.

Dave missed the elk. Not just that he didn't hit it, he didn't see it. In fairness, he did see the big smear on the road as he rode across it, but just didn't notice what was at the messy end of the smear. Really, I'm not sure how he does it. The man can focus.

We roll into Walsenburg after a glorious twenty-plus mile run of screaming tailwind and gentle descent. The only thing that could end this day and this leg of the trip better would be a good Mexican place where we can eat lunch and have a beer. Standing in the center of Walsenburg, we scan the road around us, and spot a Mexican place with neon Bud signs in the window.

Hozho.

A downhill tailwind for the last 20 miles, I feel strong and fit, it's gloriously hot out in the sun, and I have a belly full of beer and burrito.

Really, is there a better place to be in life?

26

TRANSITION

*The bicycle, the bicycle surely, should always
be the vehicle of novelists and poets.*

Christopher Morley

BETWEEN WALSENBURG AND TRINIDAD, COLORADO

We ended this leg of our trip in Walsenburg, Colorado, about 36
miles north of Trinidad, where the next leg of our trip begins.
There were logistical reasons why we chose these two points,
but they're not important. The important thing is the gap.

I've heard it said that great artists sometimes leave tiny
flaws in every work of art. The flaw emphasizes that perfection isn't part of the work we do, that everything we do can
be improved, that perfection is something that lives in God's
realm, not our realm.

While it would be silly to compare a little bike ride with
a great work of art, indulge me as I draw a tiny analogy. Art is
(or can be) very spiritual—both its creation and its enjoyment.
Art can lead us to something that we didn't even know we
needed to see, or didn't even know was there. Great art can

be a pilgrimage, either for the artist or for the person appreciating the art.

This bicycle ride was like that for me, opening perspectives that were often spiritual, leading me to places I didn't know I needed to go and people I didn't know I needed to meet. This bicycle ride led me to some of the most important things in life, things I didn't know about or understand when the ride began. It helped me discover my inner pilgrim.

The gap is my little flaw, the one I can fix any time I want. I live within a couple hours of the gap, and nearly any weekend of the year I could drive down, take a two hour bike ride, and close the gap. Cover up the flaw. If the purpose of my journey is to connect a fully contiguous path from the Pacific Ocean to the Atlantic Ocean across the U.S., this 36 mile gap from north to south would be important, and I could fix it. But the contiguous line from ocean to ocean has nothing to do with the emotional and spiritual lessons I gained while on this ride, or the people I met, or the great times I had. It has nothing to do with those most important things the bike ride led me to. This little gap reminds me of this in the same way a little flaw in a work of art reminds an artist of something similar.

Back in Sedona, I accepted the ride my friend Dale gave me headed north out of Sedona. While the road wasn't all that dangerous, and the morning was perfect for a bike ride, giving me that ride was something Dale wanted to do. Riding in the car with Dale in the predawn darkness allowed Dale to give a gift to me, it allowed him to express his friendship to me. If I'd insisted on that contiguous line rather than allowing the gift of the ride, Dale would have passed out of this life without ever having the opportunity to give that expression of friendship to me, and I would have missed the opportunity to accept that gift gracefully. We both would have been poorer for the loss.

Back in California, I skipped a few miles of particularly dangerous road, thanks to the goodness of a quirky guy who gave me a lift. Those 20 miles or so are way more valuable to me as a gap than as a deadly section of road to be traversed.

On the other side of the equation, how would I account for the extra miles I rode along the coast before heading east on my journey? Since I began riding in Monterey, which is quite a ways west of San Diego, is this ride *more than* a coast to coast ride?

What is it that's important about the *cross country* or *coast to coast* aspect of this trip? Is the trip an accounting exercise to make sure a certain number of miles is ridden? Is it a physics exercise to make sure a contiguous line is connected?

These might seem like rhetorical questions. Most of us would argue that the trip is about the journey, not an accounting exercise or a physics exercise. I'd certainly make that argument.

But inside my brain lives a nagging accountant who's busily calculating, wanting to assure that everything's connected up. He wants to make sure that if I *say* I rode my bike across the country, then the route I took connects exactly, every inch of the way. He wants to make sure I dipped my back wheel in the Pacific before I left, then dipped my front wheel in the Atlantic when I finished. I often wish I could evict this picky little bugger with the green eyeshade, but he seems to think I've invited him in, and he refuses to take a break very often.

As much as I *say* none of these picky little nits matter, the fact is they do nag me. Leaving a little 36 mile north-to-south gap here, so close to home, lets me thumb my nose at the aggravating little accounting gnome who's part of me. It forces me to accept a more holistic viewpoint of the ride. It's my way of asserting that it is, indeed, about the journey.

27

PRAIRIE DOG

If there are no dogs in Heaven, then when I die
I want to go where they went.

Will Rogers

DAY 17 • TRINIDAD TO SPRINGFIELD, COLORADO

US 160 through downtown Trinidad is deserted at 5:30 a.m.
Pedaling east in the chilly pre-dawn air, the quiet metallic purr
of my bicycle chain softly serenades me as the work warms
my muscles. A hundred yards in front of me, Dave looks like
a shadow in the darkness as he pedals, lit now and then by a
passing car, silhouetted by the faint light building along the
early dawn horizon.

While today is day 17 of our ride across the country, it's
the first day of this next leg of the journey, and the second-
longest "crossing" of our trek. For the first 75 miles of the
day, there will be no place to refill our water bottles or take
on supplies. It's not nearly as dangerous as the 90 miles across
the Mojave, but 75 miles across the high desert in July is nothing to take lightly.

Our ride today will traverse a beautiful high prairie, where the high desert of eastern Colorado rolls down toward the sweeping prairie of western Kansas. A land with great open stretches inhabited very sparsely by desert grasses, pronghorn antelope, and people steeped in toughness. I find it easy to love a place like this.

I'm not the only person who's been smitten by the beauty of the high prairie. Many readers will smile and nod as I talk about the magic of the open land and expansive skies. Those who are smiling and nodding probably grew up on the prairie, or spent formative years there. Their journey through life took them to the prairie at some point, and held them there long enough for the endless sea of grass, the big sky, and the restless wind to weave enchantment deep into their souls.

Dave has never seen this part of the country, and I feel like a young bridegroom about to introduce his best friend to his lovely bride. I'm a little worried that Dave won't find the same magic in the high plains that has enraptured me for most of my life. This is probably a bigger worry to me than the upcoming 75 miles of desolation.

The open prairie emerges in front of us, deep crimson dawn dripping across it. Ghost-like forms of old deserted homesteads take shape now and then along the horizon to our north and south. The magic of early dawn draws us down the ribbon of highway, the open prairie I call home singing me into its heart, tickling my wanderlust, caressing my thirst for adventure.

The next several days will take us through country where we're comfortable we'll be able to find motels when we need them, so we haven't set a destination for each day. Today, we have in our minds that a two hundred mile day might just be possible. Not likely, but possible if the wind is our friend. In this flat and windy country, the wind can be a very good friend, or a devastating foe.

The elusive *double century*, a checkmark I'd love to achieve at some point in my life. Could today be the day? How much do I want that checkmark? Enough to sacrifice some *smell the roses* time through this country I love so much? Enough to focus on the checkmark more than sharing this wonderful outback with my good friend?

I suppose milestones and checkmarks are always a struggle for everyone, some of us more than others. It's a little yin and yang thing. In my life, I've struggled mightily with the balance to strike between the sweet scent of roses and the addictive rush of achievement. Early in life, it cost me friendships and nearly cost me a marriage.

Intensity and focus. They can be very good things in the right dose at the right time. But in heavy doses at the wrong times, they can be lethal to maintaining good relationships, or to catching the scent of a rose. In many ways, this bicycle ride across the country is my way of testing that balance, feeling the yin, touching the yang.

As the sun climbs in the eastern sky, a ripening southeast wind on my right shoulder makes it clear that I won't need to struggle much with the yin and the yang of things today. Only a tailwind would have made the double century possible, and this isn't a tailwind beginning to blow into my right ear.

Along US 160, about 40 miles east of Trinidad, is the intersection with SH 389. On some maps, it appears that a town called Ward's Corner might have existed there at one time. Today, it's a dusty, windy spot with a structure that looks like some sort of art gallery. It doesn't appear to be open as we roll past it.

However, from behind the building, a big black dog comes galloping toward us, indicating that someone must live close by. Unlike the desert dogs back in the Mojave—the ones for whom I represented blood sport—this guy is clearly curious about us rather than threatening. Dave is 50 yards ahead of me, and I watch the dog watch Dave pass, then stand in the middle of the road staring after him. I make a little sound so he hears me coming, and he turns to watch as I approach. I have some friendly words for him, and he wags his tail. As I pedal past him, he casually turns in my direction, and begins to lope along beside me as I ride.

It's wide-open and lonely out here on the high-prairie where this guy lives. I expect he's pretty happy to have visitors come by at a pace he enjoys. It could be that he's a ranch dog who's used to riding with horses, and our bikes seem like odd horses to him. Whatever the reason, he decides we're a good pack to run with for a while. I expect him to drop off after a few hundred yards, but the further we go, the more comfortable he seems to feel beside us. The little headwind has us rolling along at an easy 12 miles per hour or so, which must be a comfortable pace for him, allowing him to fall into an easy galloping rhythm.

I'm delighted and fascinated with our new friend, and at the same time worried. He floats back and forth from one side of the road to the other, sometimes running along on the pavement right beside me, and sometimes dipping down into the ditch beside the road to run down there. While the traffic is extremely light, there is a pickup now and then that comes along one way or the other.

I feel the joy emanating from our friend as he runs with us. While I don't know the factual story of this dog, I make up a story as we sojourn together. I figure he lives on a ranch nearby, and he knows the lay of this land pretty well. Had we been cycling past his yard, he probably would have had to chase us off with a bit of growling, barking, and snapping, but since we were out in neutral territory, he's just trying to figure out who we are and what we're up to.

We look a little like a pack he might run with. Maybe it's been a while since he got to be part of a pack, to run with a pack, and scrounge with a pack, and hunt with a pack. He loves his job on the ranch, but misses the community of the pack. My friendly words as I pedal past push him over the edge. Yearning for that community, and without thinking about it, he drops into an easy gait alongside me.

Part of the pack.

The fulfillment of the community of the pack overwhelms him, and he's happy to take flank duty as we range our way down the highway. The day's not particularly hot this early in the morning, so he figures we'll be able to keep this pace up all day. A nice breeze blows in his face, and he smiles broadly as we make our way down the road.

The Pack. The joy of The Pack. The synergy of The Pack. Life is good.

A couple miles down the road, we curve off to the north a little bit, putting the wind slightly behind us, and our speed picks up a few miles an hour. Our friend drops back with our increase in speed, eventually pulling up to a stop at the side of the road, watching us disappear down the road in front of him. I look back several times as we continue to move down the road, and feel some sadness as he grows smaller and smaller along the side of the highway stretching out behind us.

We're all designed to fit within some sort of fabric. Wild dogs exist all over the world, and evolved to have a strong need to be a thread within the fabric of a pack. Different sorts of wild dogs, from wolves to coyotes to hyenas, have each evolved their own pack *texture*. As scientists have studied wolves, and come to understand the dynamics of the pack, they've been surprised to learn just how complex the fabric can be, and how much the survival and health of the animals within the pack depend on the weave and texture of the pack they live in.

In the last few thousand years, dogs have adapted to humans as humans have adapted to dogs. The "design" of the domestic dog has evolved, and domestic dogs attach themselves to their human family as a sort of pack in many ways. Dogs have learned to survive and thrive as a part of a human tribe or family. A pack.

What's the result on the well-being of the dog, I wonder? How much survives of that deep instinct to weave themselves into the fabric of a pack? Is this a strong drive deep inside the wiring of a dog? Do they feel a gap in their lives every day, an emptiness they can't understand well?

What about us, people in our culture? Are there threads that our deep wiring needs us to weave into a fabric someplace, and our inability, failure, or lack of opportunity to weave those threads into a fabric has created the same sort of gap in our lives?

It's easy to look around and see folks in our culture today, and guess that we've probably lost touch with some of those sorts of threads. I watch people around me willing to give themselves to a job for ten or twelve hours a day, shoveling their kids off to the nanny or the babysitter for 90 percent of the child's early life, knowing in their heart this is wrong, but somehow not able to find a way to re-prioritize their life and put things back in the right balance.

When the President of the United States shows this kind of dedication to his job, I'm grateful. That's important work, and lots of folks depend on him getting it right. When a talented surgeon spends 12 or 14 hours a day saving the lives of people in need, I admire that. Many dedicated folks do important work upon which people's lives depend.

However, most of us aren't protecting the free world, or saving lives with our talented hands. Most of us are simply delighted to spend hours in meetings that aren't well-run and don't need us there anyway. We're happy to spend days on internal presentations to explain things to other folks within our own company, most of whom really don't need to be involved with the issue anyway. We've created ways to make a lot of jobs seem important enough to sacrifice ourselves for. But if we really look at the value the world derives from the work, it's a bit shameful.

For this, we sacrifice what we say is most dear to us.

I'm not pointing fingers from afar; I'm as guilty as the next guy. I gave way too much of myself to my "job" in the early days, and not enough of myself to those closest to me. I get it. It's the same missing fabric issue I'm projecting onto the story I've made up about our furry friend this morning.

I could probably pick out a dozen ways to see this same

disconnect between what we say is important, and how we live our lives. I'm just picking on one I understand well.

Dangling around us in life are threads we're wired to weave into a particular sort of fabric. We're living lives that either keep us from seeing the threads, or keep us from understanding how to weave them into the kind of fabric we need. We end up doing certain things, or living certain ways, and missing the important threads in life. Our disconnected lives are a symptom of that dissonance. Most of us feel the dissonance in our lives and in our culture, but what are the real root causes?

Around each one of us are tiny threads that need us to take hold of them. The fingers of our hearts long every day to feel those threads, and the eyes of our souls long to see the pattern that is revealed as we weave those threads into a the fabric of our lives. It's the thread and the fabric I wish I could understand better.

I'm pedaling along, doing something I love to do, long-distance bicycling. When I'm doing this thing, I nearly always feel a great sense of satisfaction. There's surely a certain amount of "drug effect" from the endorphins that saturate my body when I'm riding long and hard days, but I think it's more than that. Something about this activity I love so much feels like those threads. The road and the journey feel a little like the fabric.

Christopher McDougall was a writer and a runner who wrote a book called *Born to Run*. He believed that our evolution as a species was driven, in large part, by our unique development as an endurance machine. He provides a good deal of evidence that characterizes the modern human as a species bred to run ultra-long distances.

If there's some shred of truth in the ideas that McDougall and others put forth about humans being "born to run," it explains some of the joy I get from long-distance cycling that requires a lot of endurance. This might be one of the threads I'm looking for, though I suspect it's only one of many.

Our dark-furred friend seems to have found a thread this morning. Dave and I must feel like a pack he can run with, and running with our pack weaves a thread into a fabric that feels good to him. It seems to be scratching an itch that's deep inside. Sure I'm anthropomorphizing here, but the joy in his gallop and the smile on his face are unmistakable.

28

PLACE

There's no place like home, there's no place like home . . .
L. Frank Baum, *The Wizard of Oz*

PURGATORY

The Purgatory River begins in Colorado just east of the Continental Divide near New Mexico. It runs northeast through Trinidad, then snakes through the high prairie of southeastern Colorado where it's cut some beautiful canyons over the eons. It flows into the Arkansas River around Las Animas in Colorado. The region has been called the Picket Wire region, and was home to several Native American groups before becoming part of the United States in the late 1800s. After that point, homesteaders moved in, and the bulk of the region has been in the hands of private owners since then—until recently.

In 1983, the U.S. government seized about 235,000 acres in this region to create the Piñon Canyon Maneuver Site (PCMS), or "bombing range" in common vernacular. Nearly half that land was seized using the law of eminent domain, as there were so many landowners who were "unwilling sellers."

Today, the U.S. government wants to expand that bombing range significantly, to something measured in millions of acres.

Folks in these parts are up-in-arms over this pending seizure. They don't want their land seized by a government. It's their land, and they don't want somebody else coming in and taking it from them.

Reading the signs posted on fences alongside the road as I pedal past gets me to thinking about the irony of the situation. (Is irony the right word here?) The good landowners around here are able to hold title to their land because the U.S. government seized it from the good folks who lived here 150 years ago. Nonetheless, they're up in arms over the same government seizing it *again*—only this time they're the seize-ee instead of the seize-er.

Who's right and who's wrong? Clear answers are rare. There's usually a little right and a little wrong in each point of view. Pedaling along, I'm not even thinking about the rights and wrongs of this situation. What I'm thinking about is *place*, and the importance of *place* in the lives of people. Kind of like the importance of *pack* as a thread in the existence of my black furry friend a few miles back, *place* seems to be one of those critical components to the fabric of a human life.

At the very heart of the fabric of our soul as humans is a connection we develop to a *place*. The front door of my home has a lock on it, which I use to secure my *place* from intruders. It's my home, my place, my anchor. The place where my roots are set.

At a deeper level, we want long-standing roots to a place. We feel good when we're part of a family or tribe in a *place*, and our connection to that place can sometimes reach back for generations. Just look at the ongoing enmity between Palestinians and Jews, who both claim a scrap of desert as *their place*. They're both equally right, equally wrong, and equally willing to sacrifice precious human lives to try and prove that it's more *theirs* than it is the other guy's.

I don't have any deep family roots to a place. I don't have

an ancestral home, a place where *my people* have been for generations. But I know several folks who do, and I know how much *their place* means to them.

Our culture has a definition of ownership that seems pretty unique in human history. We think we can hold onto a piece of paper, a deed, and this deed makes land ours. This way of thinking about land ownership presents problems to most of us as we try to understand how people have historically looked at *place*, and how they fit into it.

Two hundred years ago, this land I'm riding across today was part of a border region between several nations of people: to the southeast, the vast Comanche Nation; to the north and east, the Kiowa, Cheyenne, and others; to the west and northwest, the Ute, and to the southwest, the Apache and others. They had no *deed* for their land, but each nation in its own way felt kinship with and attachment to their *place*. It was their home. They were part of it and it was part of them. Their religious beliefs were often woven into their understanding of how the universe put them here and gave them this *place*.

This theme isn't unique to the people of this land. Think of the ancient Hebrews and their connection to the land of Israel. They believed (and believe) that God put them in that place, and "gave them" the place, that they are part of the place and the place is part of them.

It's a common theme with humans. We like to be part of a place, and to have that place be part of us. *Place* quickly becomes sacred to us, and we wrap God up in our place, and make God part of the relationship between us and *our place*.

I have favorite hunting spots I've developed over the years. While I don't own the land, I've come to know a great deal about the land and everything that lives on it. Year to year, I watch specific animals as they mature, and I see how the animals use the territory a little differently each year. I feel a part of the place, and I feel the place is part of me. When I share it with a hunting buddy, I feel like I'm sharing something very sacred.

Pedaling through this high prairie land that feels so much like the prairie where I spent my formative years, I feel a strong connection to the place. The bicycle gives me a closeness to the road and the wind and the heat that I couldn't get in a motorized vehicle, enhancing my connection to the place, weaving the thread more tightly.

I realize, with a smile on my face, that these next several days will take me through *my place*. I don't hold any deeds to any property along the way, but my heart and soul know this as *my place*. Weaving this thread into the fabric of my life today might be one of the lessons I need to learn in the saddle of this journey.

29

SANTA FE TRAIL

I am beginning to learn that it is the sweet, simple things of life which are the real ones after all.

Laura Ingalls Wilder

PRITCHETT, COLORADO

Kim, Colorado is a little spot on the road between one curve and the next, with a general store and not much else. For Dave and me, after 75 miles of saddle-time with a little more headwind than we'd hoped for, there's a palpable uplift to our spirits as we see the town coming into sight from a few miles up the road.

The air conditioning in the general store, along with a deli sandwich and lots of fluid, feel good to both the spirit and the body. We chat with some bikers—the kind who wear leather and ride cycles that make lots of noise and go fast. I delight again in the two-wheeled camaraderie we share—fellow travelers out on the desert highway. We take off a bit before they do, and when they overtake us a few miles down the road, they wave and hoot and holler as they speed by.

This highway we're on today was laid down along the path of the old Santa Fe Trail, or at least parts of it were. Before we called it the Santa Fe Trail, other folks before us used the trail as a trading route between cultures separated by hostile landscapes. This morning, I feel like one of those early adventurers along this trail, sharing a wave and a hoot and a holler with some fellow adventurers along an ancient trail, sharing the beauty up-close and personal, feeling the heat, tasting the wind.

About 15 miles west of Springfield is a little dot on the map called Pritchett. An old prairie town that feels desolate and deserted today. I imagine it was hurt badly in the late 1920s and early 1930s when most of the prairie towns were devastated by the one-two punch of economic disaster and the Dust Bowl. Based on the map, I didn't expect to find anything in Pritchett. Rolling through what appears to be the old deserted downtown square, I'm surprised when Dave pulls over at a cafe sign. There's one old truck in front of the building, but nothing else anywhere downtown. Dave hollers over to me that it looks like they've got ice cream.

Ice cream? Really? Here in the middle of nowhere? A gift from the universe.

Life is good.

I wheel around, pull up to the hitchin' post, and head in. I'm still feeling that connection to the trail riders of olden days, only instead of the dry dusty jingle of spurs as I reach for the door, there's the tap tap of cleats on the concrete, and the swoosh swoosh of spandex. Still . . .

Inside we meet Kathi, the proprietor, who scoops us some ice cream. We sit and chat with her and her husband Steve about their diner and their business. They're new to the area. They've been pleasantly surprised by the friendly reception they've gotten in town, and how well the local folks support their diner. They're open for breakfast and lunch, then on Friday nights for dinner. Sitting at the table, chatting with Steve and Kathi and soaking in the AC while savoring cold ice cream,

I sincerely hope they'll be successful in the long run here in this little town.

What draws folks to dusty old towns like Pritchett, and motivates them to make a go of it? It's a lot like the truck farm folks we met back in western Colorado. If you sit down with pencil and paper, I can't imagine you can make a viable business plan that would justify pulling up roots and moving yourself out into these desolate high plains. But in the case of Steve and Kathi, that's exactly what they've done. They raised a family on traditional jobs in more traditional cities, then decided it was time to pull up stakes and start over again in the tiny little town of Pritchett, Colorado. They have a little diner called the Pritchett Café, and Kathi sells antiques and other little stuff in the shop next door called the Blue Willow Trading Company. They also own an old house in town that they're renovating and will run as a B&B soon.

Slowly finishing my ice cream, I gaze out onto the deserted street as they tell me their story. They're obviously bright and hardworking folks with good common sense. What compelled them to make the move they made? I can't come up with the right words to ask the question without having it sound wrong, so I just listen as they talk about the life they led while raising their family, and how much they enjoy the life they're leading today.

There's a quiet, unchanging permanence that's part of the chord you hear in the wind that blows through the high prairie. The dry wind parching the land, the hard sun blazing in the sky, the brutal winter storms venting their fury across the sagebrush. To live here, you've got to accept those layers and complexions that define this place. You've got to feel the peace in the quiet, hear the harmony in the chords of the wind, find the beauty in wide and desolate places.

There's clearly a strong sense of place to the high prairie, an allure. Not everyone hears it, but for those who do, it's a powerful song that draws them out into the open space. I know the song. I hear it in my soul. I think it's part of what drew me to this particular route when planning the trip, a chance to spend more time in this place that feels like the center of the world to me. I recognize the same thing in others now and again, folks like Steve and Kathi.

Will they be able to make a go of it here in Pritchett? My logical brain doubts it as I watch the wind blowing the dust in the empty street outside. The center of my soul is drawn strongly to the open space that is this *High Prairie Place*, and regardless of my logical brain, I want very much for them to be successful.

30

STAGE STOP HOTEL

Heaven goes by favor. If it went by merit, you would stay out and your dog would go in.

Mark Twain

CHERRY

Approaching Springfield, Dave and I both admit defeat of our hope for a 200 mile day. I've unexpectedly developed some blazing saddle sores, and I really want to get my butt out of the saddle. My legs have more miles in them, but my butt's done for the day. Bittersweet.

I let the disappointment wash out of me as we ride into Springfield. By the time we hit downtown, I'm completely fine with stopping, and want no part of going on. My mind is now 100 percent done, and I'm already letting myself feel those sores I've been trying to ignore.

We ride past a neat looking old place called the Stage Stop Hotel, but notice the "No Vacancy" sign in the window. There are a couple motels on the north side of town, so we ride on. My body is already soaking in the promise of a hot shower, and my stomach is starting to ponder the menu it hopes to find at the steak house in town. Pulling up to the first motel we come to, we go in and ask about a room. We're devastated to find out that not only are they full, but there's some sort of rodeo event in town this weekend, so every room in town is booked. The guy behind the desk makes a couple calls for us just to make sure, and our heads are hangin' mighty low when we walk back outside to face the prospect of another 50 miles in the saddle to the next town with a motel.

Riding back toward US 160, the wind in my face is a bitter reminder of what I've got to look forward to for the next three or four hours. Riding past the old Stage Stop Hotel, I suggest to Dave that we should stop and ask anyway. I know the sign says, "No Vacancy," and I know the guy at the last hotel called to make sure they're full, but I'm thinking we should stop and ask.

Dave agrees. We pull up to the hitching post in front (really) and dismount. Our dismounts have less vigor with each passing hour, and I'm really hoping this is my last for the day. I really want there to be a room here. We drag ourselves up the steps and open the front door. "Hi," we start up, "we know you say you don't have any vacancy, but we were wondering if you . . ."

A woman about our age cuts us off before we can finish. "I've got a room with two beds, and it's waiting for you."

The weight of the world lifts from my shoulders, and I sit down in the shade of the front porch while Dave signs us in. Cherry Gonser, the proprietor, says to Dave that she thinks God brought us together. Dave figures that she might just be really picky about who she rents to, and keeps the "No Vacancy" sign on so she can size up potential tenants before deciding to rent them a room. It could also be that she just got a cancellation before we walked in the door. And it absolutely could be just as Cherry says: God was watching over a couple of worn-out middle-aged guys, making sure Cherry held that last room open for us.

On a bench in the shade in front of Cherry's hotel, feeling pure bliss at our good fortune in having a place for the night, a little bubble of joy surrounds me as I watch the small town evening unfolding on the high prairie in front of me. This is truly a moment for me to enjoy, and I'm very grateful.

Whether God really did make this hotel room happen for Dave and me today isn't important to me. If you believe God's hand is present in everything that happens, then one way or another the hand of God helped us find lodging tonight. Or maybe it's as simple as dumb luck, and Cherry decided Dave and I looked like upstanding enough citizens that she was willing to rent to us.

What is important is the joy and contentment I feel right now. How thankful and grateful I am to have a place to stop for the night, relax and clean up, enjoy a great dinner, and allow my body to recover for the next day.

Right there—in this moment wrapped up in joy, contentment, and thanks—that's where I find something some folks call divine. Maybe the edge of this glimmer is what Cherry saw when she decided Dave and I were the reason she'd been saving that room.

SPRINGFIELD, CO

THE GREAT PLAINS

Medicine Lodge, KS

31

HARMONY

In the house made of dawn.
In the story made of dawn.
On the trail of dawn,
May their roads home be on the trail of peace,
Happily may they all return,
In beauty I walk.
With beauty before me, I walk.

Part of a Navaho chant

DAY 18 · SPRINGFIELD, COLORADO TO PLAINS, KANSAS

Pre-dawn twilight, a south wind rippling up a quiet and deserted Main Street. Dave and I lean against our bikes, taking in fluid and calories. Some flavor of a kind westerly wind, and we have a chance to make 150 miles to Meade, Kansas. Climbing into the saddle, we make our way through town and east along US 160.

A breathtaking sunrise builds and unrolls in the eastern sky, shining into our eyes as our tires roll silently along the glass-smooth pavement below us. A tiny breeze blows against my back, bringing a smile to my face. This must be about as wonderful as a human being can feel. Settling into a nice pace, listening to the morning birds on the prairie around me, I enjoy the stellar little slice of life that I'm lucky enough to be traveling through this morning.

Let's talk wind.

Wind resistance is the biggest obstacle a cyclist has to overcome as he rolls down the road. Reducing wind resistance means you travel farther and faster for the same amount of work. A common way that cyclists reduce wind resistance is to form a paceline, riding in a line, each rider taking advantage of the rider(s) in front. In this way, the riders taking advantage of the slipstream reduce their effort by 30 percent or more.

There's both art and science to making a paceline work.

The *science* component of making this happen is pretty straightforward. Simply said, riding in a paceline (or drafting) is the process of riding a straight line at a steady speed, very closely together. Since wheels are often only inches apart, the tiniest changes to speed or direction can result in unwelcome, rapid, and intimate contact with the pavement.

If a group of riders all have strength that's relatively close to each other, then everyone takes their short turn at the front doing the hard work, then rotates to the back of the line. The process continues ad-infinitum, allowing the group as a whole to cover significantly more miles for the work expended. The group goes a lot farther in a given day than they would have been able to if everyone worked alone. Two or three riders of unequal strength fall into a rotation where the strongest in the group take the longest turns in the front doing the work. The result is the same: the group as a whole makes it much farther and faster on the same amount of work. The beauty of efficiency.

Which brings us to the *art* of the paceline First, I find grace and beauty in efficiency, and a paceline is a tangible, palpable manifestation of this grace and beauty. Second, in order to make it work effectively, there's a great deal of unspoken connection that's required between the riders in the line. The riders need to tune into their unconscious mind, and connect at that level with one another. There's great art in this deep harmonious connection.

It's a lot like singing a cappella with a small group of folks. I've sung with other folks, and have come to realize that I have a voice that's barely passable. But my voice blends with other voices well. The result can be something beyond nice, it can be a beautiful work of art and synergy that's a completely new voice. Each of us by ourselves might be just okay, but when we lean together, finding the sweet spot where one voice fills in the blanks that another voice might have, finding the perfect pitch to work as a harmony... It can be a thing of profound beauty, sending chills down my spine and spreading a smile of deep satisfaction and wonder across my face.

Synergy. The whole is greater than the sum of the parts.

Something magical grows out of harmony in practice and application. In the case of a cycling paceline, harmony and efficiency come together in a way that you feel in every pedal stroke. Deep focus on the line as a whole, and how it is that you fit into the line, is required. You need to be in close touch with how you apply work to the pedals in order to maintain exactly the right pace at every moment. Deeply satisfying when it's working well, risky if you take your eye off the ball. Within yourself, your mind and body are in tune, and every individual is in tune with the paceline as an entity.

It's a beautiful thing when it works well.

Dave's not sure. In my mind, his aversion to drafting is just a matter of getting comfortable with the idea. I'm positive that once he tries it and starts to gain comfort with it, he'll see and feel the beauty in the harmony and efficiency. Even if he never feels comfortable drafting behind me, by learning to ride at the front and let me draft behind him, he'll be able to set a faster pace most of the time because I'll then be able to keep up with that faster pace.

Dave's a logical guy. Dave loves efficiency as much as I do. This is a no-brainer to me, we'll be drafting one way or another by the end of today. I'm sure of it. It's obvious.

Like the old saying goes, "What's obvious to you, is obvious to you . . ."

While Dave and I both find joy in riding, the places where joy reveals itself are quite different between us. Dave doesn't like holding a steady pace or position on the bike. He likes to vary his pace, stand up for a few pedal strokes, then sit back down on the saddle; get down in the drops, then back on the tops. These are not riding habits that lend themselves to making a paceline work successfully, but it's how Dave likes to ride.

I've got to be careful about riding beside Dave. He's stronger than I am, and is probably trying to make sure he doesn't set a pace that's too fast for me. When I ride up beside him, he's wondering if I'm trying to go a little faster. So he goes faster, and I try to keep up, and he goes faster, I try to keep up, la la la. Infinite acceleration loop.

So this morning, I look for the right opportunity to slip up behind Dave and settle in to his draft, hoping that if I stay right behind him, he won't think I'm trying to push the pace up.

I wait until the road eases toward the northeast, so the wind is a little more behind our right shoulders. It's a bit trickier drafting in a crosswind, because the slipstream isn't directly behind the rider in front, but off to one side. The stronger and more direct the crosswind, the farther off to the side it is. I want to be more behind Dave than beside him, so he doesn't start his infinite acceleration loop.

I ease up behind Dave, a little off to his left, and find his slipstream. My front wheel is several inches to the left of Dave's back wheel, and overlaps just a bit. Being a little to his left lets me see up the road as I ride. I find the right gear, and settle into a comfortable cadence. Dave keeps looking over his shoulder at me, but I'm used to that now, and figure that as we settle into a rhythm, he'll become more comfortable that he's not leaving me behind, and I'm not trying to go faster.

I'm feeling good. I'm thinking we'll develop the magical harmony like this, and Dave will find the joy in it, and pretty soon he'll be comfortable drafting behind me as well. He'll see the beauty, and feel the harmony, and the joy will touch him. I'm smiling; it's just a matter of time now.

We're moving along, dropping into a healthy pace, when Dave suddenly sits up and drops his speed. Normally, this would cause instant crash behind, as the guy behind would run into your back wheel if he wasn't expecting a change in pace. But this morning, it's not a problem, since I'm off to his left. I ease up alongside and glance over at him. It's clear that he's not winded, and I don't really think that he wants me to do the pulling, so I just ride beside him until he seems to drop back down and start a steady pedaling, at which time I ease in behind him on his left again, find that sweet spot in the draft, and settle into our rhythm again.

And again, just as I'm feeling like we're approaching that sweet harmony and rhythm, Dave sits up and drops a couple miles an hour. Again, I ease up beside him and we ride side by side for a while, and after a couple minutes he drops back down and we do the whole thing over.

After three or four rounds of this, I figure maybe he wants me to pull for a while. When he sits up, I ease around him on the left, and pull over for him to fall in behind me. While I can't keep Dave's pace up for long, I figure I can hold it for a few minutes, then rotate back, and we can develop a pattern that works.

But looking in my mirror, I see that Dave isn't sitting in my draft or anywhere close to it. So I drop the pace back, figuring he'll pass. Eventually he does pass, and then I drop in behind him, and we start the whole yo-yo process again. We go through this pattern several times before we hit some new chip seal surface. The surface is so rough that drafting isn't really an option, so I drop back and relax while Dave pulls ahead.

The chip seal ends after five miles or so, but we've both had enough of trying to make a paceline work. Clearly, a paceline just isn't Dave's cup of tea. Riding along, I'm able to let this soak in, and teach me a simple lesson, one that probably seems obvious to most folks.

Joy and beauty aren't universal truths. Oh sure, we each have the ability to find joy, and to appreciate beauty, but we find them in different places. An obvious joy to me is just a hassle to the next guy.

Not only does Dave not find the pure joy that I find in the harmony of a paceline, but more basic is the fact that our riding styles are dramatically different. In my case, I love that sweet spot of exertion and gearing where my heart-rate, respiration rate, and cadence seem in perfect tune, and I can go and go and go. Once I find it, I feel like I can go for hours. To me, that's nirvana on a bike.

Dave, on the other hand, likes to change things up. He likes to vary his cadence, and his position, and his effort. He likes to vary them pretty often. This feels good to him, and allows him to maintain interest in the pedaling.

This difference in style would drive each of us nuts if we let it, as we've both discovered this morning. By mid-morning, we've gone back to our pattern where Dave gets ahead on the road, and varies his pace however he wants. I find a steady pace, and just hold it, knowing that Dave will yo-yo somewhere out in front of me, but I'll generally stay within a few hundred yards of him.

Dave wonders if this is another example of his theory that I find more joy in the world than he does. I don't think so. I think it's one more example of how we find joy differently. We're both riding and we're both enjoying the ride. It's just that forcing either of us to try to find the *same joy* in the *same way* as the other would be a disaster. It robs us of the joy we *do* find.

Obvious . . .

32

WESTERN KANSAS

Our Bible is the wind.

Plains Indian proverb

LAND OF THE SOUTH WIND

Dave and I leave our bikes leaning against the front window of the lonely diner in downtown Johnson City, Kansas, finding respite from the steady and growing 25 knot wind ripping down the main street. We've ridden 50 miles this morning before breakfast, and averaged 20 miles per hour. We're feelin' good as we wolf down a pair of double cheeseburgers. We know that when we saddle back up and head east, that south wind will be working hard to blow us right off our bikes and across the highway. The infamous Kansas wind is about to put an end to our fun this morning.

The origin of the name "Kansas" isn't certain, though most scholars believe its root is in a common word used by tribes in the area. The Siouan word "Kansa" referred to a tribe that lived in the area, and roughly translated to something like "People of the South Wind" or "Wind" or "Swift Wind" or "Wind People" or "Land of the South Wind." There's also a less credible assertion that the word has a Spanish root, translating into something relating to the idea of disturbing or stirring up, generally referring to a group of people. The folks who buy this theory believe the name was given by the early Spanish explorers to the area, back in 1541, to refer to the tribes that harassed them (or stirred things up) along their trail. Again, this theory isn't very widely accepted.

Anyone who's spent any time in Kansas will go with the "swift wind" origin. Leaving the diner and heading straight east, Dave and I are harassed and disturbed by a swift wind pounding across our starboard. By the time we reach Ulysses, it takes significant effort to keep from being blown over by a brutal crosswind ripping at us from the south.

A McDonald's offers us a great excuse to escape the wind for a few minutes. The wind buffets the windows and tries to rip the flag off the pole at the Deere dealership across the street as we quietly consume some ice cream. The wind is only going to get worse as the day progresses, so we're back out in the gale after a brief 15 minutes in the shelter of McDonald's.

I read an article once about a study done to find out what piece of high-performance gear had the most positive effect on the ability of the cyclist to go faster. Cycling companies are always trying to come up with super high-tech fabrics for shorts and jerseys, special aerodynamic covers for shoes, special helmet shapes, not to mention the thousands that they'd like you to spend on highly tuned bicycle frames and components. Funny thing they discovered in this study: one of the most significant performance improvements came from an unlikely piece of gear—ear plugs that cut out the sound of the wind.

I've never considered myself much of an aficionado when it comes to cursing. In fact, I'm barely a practitioner. My sons were in their late teens before they realized I even knew how to curse. But there's something about riding with a strong wind ripping through my ears that sucks the curses out of some dark place in my soul.

We're deep into wheat country now, surrounded by a sea of golden wheat ripening in rolling yellow waves beneath a bright blue Kansas sky. Spring and early summer wrap Kansas in mystical oceans of wheat, and I find them endlessly mesmerizing. The graceful feel of a bright golden field of wheat when it's ripe, rolling in waves beneath the wind, makes the world feel big and bright with soft edges. Even after it's been cut, it has a warm feel to it.

It's become more humid as our journey has taken us east, and humid air carries scent more effectively than dry air. A stretch of road runs right up against a field of corn seven feet tall on our right, providing a pretty decent windbreak for us. The wind rushing over the tops of our heads drops the scent of ripe corn across us as we ride. The strong and sweet smell floods my mind with memories of sweet corn in the summer, spending time as a little boy working with my grandpa in his garden on hot afternoons, the squeaky sound of fresh corn as the husk is ripped off, the sweet yellow smell exploding in my face.

This memory is a little glass of sweetness in an ocean of bitter wind. Images of Grandpa's face, and the faces of others I associate with him, flood my mind's eye as I pedal in the lee of the towering cornfield. I see my mother's smile as she considers the corn in front of her on the table. I feel myself at my grandparents' little home, and out in Grandpa's big garden.

Few things in life are as powerful in the mind as smell, and I cherish that power for a few miles of hot Kansas highway riding, sheltered from a ripping wind.

Swinging out of our saddles at a convenience store in Satanta, we grab our empty water bottles and duck inside for another brief respite from the wind. It's something north of 95 degrees, and the wind has to be a steady 40 knots or more. The heat has drained any appetite from us, so we share a tube of Pringles potato chips while relaxing at a table, taking in fluid.

The astute reader will note at this point that we're 100 miles into the day, and I've taken in one cheeseburger, one ice cream cone, and now half a tube of potato chips. Ignore for a minute the poor *quality* of the calories, and smile at the low *quantity* of calories. I'm headed toward a dark corner of the world that every cyclist fears and loathes. I'll name that dark corner in a few paragraphs, but for now suffice it to say that it creeps toward me in the cool of the convenience store..

Dave and I enjoy some good conversation with the old folks hanging out at the store. They're all older than us, most of them are old enough to be our parents. A couple old fellas tell us all about a brother who used to ride bikes, and a nephew who still does. We talk about where we're from and where we're headed. They've got plenty of good and detailed advice about the road ahead.

The thing that strikes Dave and me most is their concern, their genuine and heartfelt concern, for our safety and well-being. They're careful to make sure we've got plenty of ice in our water bottles, and that we've been drinking enough water. They tell us the places on the road where we've got to be particularly careful.

This genuine concern for our well-being is a recurring theme that Dave and I will experience on this old highway across Kansas. You grow accustomed to the way most metropolitan folks say words of pseudo caring without the true underlying deep concern. I do it myself, ask folks how they're doing but I really don't want any long answers, tell folks to take care but it's just the polite thing to say.

On this hot and windy afternoon in Satanta, this group of old folks gathered at the convenience store really cares about our safety and well-being. Truly, honestly, and from the heart.

It feels very good.

Swinging into the saddle, we resume our struggle with the wind as it pounds across us, then turn south again into the teeth of the wind. After five miles or so that feels like it takes an hour to traverse, we come to a little turnout where we rest before turning east again. "Rest" is probably not the best word for the few minutes we spend standing there in the shade at the turnout, as the wind continues its relentless assault while we take in fluids and a few calories. Well, Dave takes in both fluid and calories, while I drink water but seem oblivious to the serious calorie debt to my body I've been building all day. I eat nothing at all.

This is the place where you, the reader, begin to hear dark and scary music barely audible in the background. A dark and loathsome corner of hell is sneaking up on me as I ride east. While I might catch a corner of a shadow of that darkness as it rapidly gains on me, I ignore it with callous arrogance. When it finally catches me, it sweeps through me like a horde of emptiness, sucking all but the most meager ability to produce work out of my reach.

Bonk.

It happens fast. The dark little tentacles of bonkness wrap themselves around my legs, and I'm happy when Dave pulls over for a quick drink. I eat a couple crackers I have in my bag, thinking this might stem the tide of darkness that's rapidly engulfing me. There's some GU Energy Gel in the bag too, something that might replenish the calorie debt quickly, but for some inexplicable reason I don't eat that.

Dave's worn-out from the day, but was smarter about taking in a few more calories, avoiding the dark corner of misery into which I rapidly descend. We're only a couple miles from Plains, and we agree that if there's a motel in town, we'll stop for the night rather than pushing on the next dozen or so miles to Meade. The dark bonk has engulfed me deeply enough that I feel barely coherent, hearing only vague concepts somewhere on the other side of the edge of my darkness.

My body is shutting itself down as we ride into Plains, and my brain doesn't even know how to wonder why it's suddenly so stupid. Downtown is deserted as we stop on a corner to get out our cheat-sheet with the hotel numbers in all the small towns. We must look way worse than we feel (which says a lot right now), because a lady goes out of her way to drive up to us and ask us if we need anything. She points us to the motel, which stands just a block away in plain sight to anyone with a functioning brain. She also tells us about the bar in town, which is also the only place that serves food, and only serves steaks on Saturday nights. Disappointment takes hold of me for a few seconds as a steak sounds wondrously good right now, but then the disappointment fades as my brain catches up to the fact that it's Saturday night . . .

Here it is again. This genuine concern that a complete stranger has for us. This lady drove past us, then turned around and drove back to talk to us. I give you my money-back guarantee this was not flirting; we're two old guys who look like hell and smell worse. This was pure concern for the well-being of another human being. She offers to drive us to anywhere we need to go, but really, we're a block away from where we need to end up.

Coasting up to the hotel, my arms are shaking uncontrollably and my eyes are struggling to focus. All I can do is sit in a chair outside the office while Dave checks us in to the hotel. This is the second time in my life I've bonked, falling off this ledge, watching helplessly as my brain begins shutting itself down due to lack of glycogen in the tank, which is the fuel the brain runs on. I don't ever want to see a third time.

Some energy gel soaks into me as I lay on the bed waiting for Dave to finish his shower, giving me enough fuel to shower, dress and walk over to the bar, where the consumption of large quantities of calories begins. A very large steak, a baked potato piled with everything they could find in the fridge, some sort of green vegetable that I don't take the time to notice as I toss it past my lips and down my gullet, and very large quantities of water bring my brain fully back to life and begin to soak into my body. Beer would be a good thing to avoid. I don't avoid it. Dave and I review the day and the ride so far over a couple rounds of Bud. Over the period of an hour or so, the day has transformed itself into a wonderful evening with a very dear friend. I'm sure it helped that the waitress was quite easy on the eyes. It always does.

33

THE BIG TABLE

*Love one another, but make not a bond of love: Let it
rather be a moving sea between the shores of your souls.*
Kahlil Gibran

DAY 19 • PLAINS TO COLDWATER, KANSAS

We're a refreshed couple of human beings Sunday morning,
standing outside the local convenience store, wolfing down
calories in the pre-dawn twilight. Our water bottles are topped
off with ice water, and our strength is back up to 100 percent.
The southwest wind has been up before dawn, ready to push
us up US 54 to Meade.

US 54 from Plains to Meade reminds us of what we don't
like about roads for biking. Traffic.

On the one hand there's an argument for using primary
highways that have wide shoulders with plenty of room for
cars to pass. This approach keeps you closer to civilization,
with more access to supplies. On the other hand is the argument for secondary and tertiary roads that have low traffic
levels, even if that means a smaller (or non-existent) shoulder.
Both approaches work.

If you check out route advice on the web, you'll most likely be shown routes like US 54 as good bicycle routes. Depending on why you're on the bike pedaling down the highway, and what you hope to get out of the trip, it might be the right approach. You've got to ask yourself what the trip's about, and what you're looking to find along the route.

I'm not able to enjoy the beautiful sunrise unfolding around me for all the crap in the shoulder and heavy truck traffic as we ride along US 54, finally rolling into Meade. The 12 mile ride reminds me, once again, of why I'm pedaling my bike down the highway. Highways that are well travelled just aren't worth the tradeoff for me. They're too busy, loud, and full of fumes. The shoulder is more a hindrance than a help, as I dodge the glass and metal and who knows what else.

Rolling into Meade as the sun breaks the horizon, we're treated to a small town at dawn. This brings to our minds the small-town diner, and we're both looking for this place as we pedal through town. It's a place along the downtown strip with big windows. A place that's been there forever, helping to define the town. A big table in the back of the room is full of men sipping coffee and socializing before heading back out the door to their day. The food's tolerable, and the waitress knows everyone by first name. There's a stack of menus someplace, but nobody uses them at breakfast, since the waitress knows what everybody wants and only asks as a pleasantry.

The small-town diner.

I maintain a fondness for the small-town diner at breakfast time. At that big table somewhere close to the back there's a well-defined but unspoken pecking order and structure, defining who sits where. Guys come and go as the morning rolls along; seems like about the time one guy leaves, another walks through the front door and takes a seat. A woman would never sit at that table, nor would a stranger in town. This is the morning gathering place, where men socialize, then it's off to chores at the farm or the store in town.

The big table's a social place, where good-natured jabs are traded, talk of futures prices and rain chances are common, and the bonds that hold a community together are reinforced each morning as the day begins. I imagine women have their spots as well, places where local bonds are molded and reinforced, but it's just not something I'm tuned into. The big table at the local diner is something I've been fascinated with most of my life. There's an energy that happens there in that *place* in town. It's one of the sources of energy that holds a town together, and holds a people together. Surely not the only source, but an important one.

Dave and I ride clean through town to the other side, looking down the side streets, but see no evidence of the local diner. Dejectedly, we turn around and ride to the truck stop we passed on the west edge of town. It's still a small town, so folks at the truck stop know each other, and are friendly in a small town way.

But there's no big table. I don't get the sense from the patrons that this is *their place*. This place lacks that important energy that comes from the locally owned small town diner. There's none of that important glue that's distilled and shared at the big table in that diner.

A community is knit together by threads that come from places like the local hardware store, the local grocery, and the local diner. Without this energy, without this glue, without these threads, the local diner sits empty and abandoned as the wind blows down Main Street in the morning all by itself.

Diligent today to avoid the hellish conclusion that yesterday's bonk rained down on me, I have a hearty breakfast that includes a giant slab of chicken-fried steak, some eggs, toast, potatoes, and whatever Dave leaves on his plate. Funny how pain brings focus. Yesterday I rolled along all day, not missing the calories I wasn't taking in. The pain of a total bonk zeroed my focus on those missed calories, and the need to avoid the pain again sits in the front of my mind as I devour calories at the breakfast table. If only I could have thought about this a little bit yesterday before it got too late. By the time I recognized the unraveling that was happening within me, it was too late. The spiral downward had started, and the pain of the bonk was unstoppable.

Back in the saddle and pedaling east through town again, I think about my unraveling yesterday, about the signs that were there all through the day that I ignored, and I hope we catch the unraveling of our culture before it's too late. I hope we learn to support local businesses rather than driving to the Walmart 20 miles away. I hope we learn to eat at the local diner rather than the big chain restaurant. Glancing down the streets, my heart breaks for the slow unraveling of towns like this. The big table is quiet, behind a dusty and abandoned window that's been boarded up for a few years now.

34

COMANCHE ROLLERS

*I was born on the prairie where the wind blew free
and there was nothing to break the light of the sun.*

Geronimo

MEATLOAF AND HEAT

US 160 forks right and eases away from US 54 just east of
town. We glide atop the silky smooth asphalt, nudged along by
a growing tailwind, delighted by the growing distance between
us and US 54. The incessant hum of truck tires is replaced by
the feathery rustle of the grass around us under the soft urging
of the breeze. Meadowlarks sing their lonely plainsong across
the prairie, gurgling and trickling across the top of the grass
in liquid melodies. The quiet magic of the great prairie wraps
itself around me. The peace of the rolling sea of grass slowly
reaches inside my soul, edging out my melancholy over the
loss of the big table.

A pair of marsh hawks glide low across the prairie, skip-
ping over the top of the rolling sea of grass. Their ancestors
skipped along the top of these waves for far longer than my ancestors sat at the big table. Marsh hawks surfed these hills when

the great Comanche Nation ruled the plains on their mighty fleets of ponies. They soared over this sea of grass for eons before that, when people we know nothing about lived here.

Cultures come and go. People come and go. We all want to believe we're special, like we've finally got it figured out and the world is lucky to have us. But the marsh hawk glides on, finding his rodents, raising his offspring, surfing the wind. He adapts to a changing table.

The deep hilly grassland we're riding through this morning was once the northern fringe of the Comanche world. The flat farmland of 50 miles back, plowed and irrigated, has been replaced with big rolling hills covered in grass and cattle. I feel transported in time, riding along on two wheels like a Comanche warrior might have ridden along this trail on a horse. He'd be looking out over rolling hills covered in buffalo, elk, and antelope instead of the steady diet of cattle I'm watching.

But the marsh hawks would be surfing low across the hills just like they are today. Meadowlarks would be singing him down the trail with the same notes that make up the sweet serenade I hear as I pedal my steed down the asphalt trail. The small group of deer would still watch from the edge of the creek-bottom, where the sea of grass is briefly punctuated by the occasional tree.

Some things change, some things stay the same. Driven along the road by the wind behind me, serenaded by meadowlarks on either side of the trail, watched by the occasional marsh hawk above, I'm enjoying the things that stay the same. The Comanche were part of this *place*, and it was part of them. This morning, I feel a tiny thread of connection to the magic of that kinship.

Historians today say the Comanche Nation lost their *place* to invaders who had greater numbers and greater technology. Of course, the historians who say this come from the culture that won. We rarely hear what historians would say who come from the losing side when cultures clash.

I wonder what historians will say 200 years from now, when they look back and lament the loss of the big table. Will they say we let our Rural Nation slip through our hands like the wind moves through the grass? Diner by diner, hardware store by hardware store, they'll map the demise of a once-great People. Will the sea of grass still be here then? Will the marsh hawk still hunt rodents? Will the song of the meadowlark be as sweet?

A gloriously beautiful morning blooms all around me, and the universe feels vital and clean and fresh. My heart's happy to be here. A swift tailwind propels me down the highway. Infused with strength and vigor, I power up the hills in a big gear. A happy heart, a smiling soul, and legs that feel strong.

Life is good this morning.

Approaching Big Basin, the highway bends south, subjecting us to a quartering headwind for five or six miles before turning again to the east. As the wind moves around from my face to my back, the smile on my face returns to its proper upright position. Dave finds what must be the only tree along the 70 miles of road between Meade and Coldwater, and we pull over to enjoy a little respite from the late morning heat. Just like fish and wildlife, we're attracted to the "structure," and can't resist stopping to enjoy the tiny ten square feet of shade.

Stopping at the Ranch House Cafe in Ashland, the proprietor is just laying out the buffet for the Sunday church crowd. The air conditioning is cool, the food is plentiful and good, and I'm hungry. My sense of drive to consume calories is encouraged, I'm sure, by my bonk experience of the day before. Notwithstanding lessons learned in the past about large quantities of fatty foods when bicycling in hot weather, we dig in to a wonderful second breakfast that includes a couple heaping plates of hot meatloaf.

It'll be 30 minutes too late when I remember why shoveling two big plates of meatloaf and mashed potatoes into my belly before going out and pedaling down the burning asphalt on a hot July Kansas day isn't the wisest thing a guy can do. Now, the astute reader will recall that this isn't the first of these sorts of food and heat debacles I've recounted in this story.

It won't be the last either. This is a lesson I seem incapable of learning.

Leaving the cafe, filling our bottles with ice and water at the convenience store in town, we look at each other with great disappointment as we realize that our wonderful west wind has now died—there isn't a breath of air moving. With no breeze to move the heat off the surface of the blacktop, the temperature soars to 109 as we roll down the road.

This is the point, by the way, where I'm regretting that second plate of meat loaf and mashed potatoes.

35

THE SOUL OF A PLACE

*The best portion of a good man's life—his little,
nameless, unremembered acts of kindness and love.*
William Wordsworth

AIRBORNE RODEO

Our quick break at the convenience store in the little town
of Protection is really just an excuse to sit in some air conditioning. We're passing through country now with which I feel
a very strong kinship, a sense of *place* and connection. I've
hunted birds and deer on this land for years, spending count-
less hours of quiet time in the open fields and hedgerows close
to here, communing with the rhythm of the land, learning the
songs and patterns of the wildlife. My connection with this
place grows each time I hunt here.

The connection isn't an *ownership* thing. There are many
places where I feel this connection, some on private land owned
by someone else, some on public land. The sense of connection
I'm talking about actually belies the entire notion of "ownership" of land in many ways.

If I had been a land and slave owner 200 years ago in the America that supported slavery, how would I have felt toward people I *owned*? Just how much would I have felt that a slave was really mine? My apologist mind likes to think I'd have considered the labor of this person to be *mine*, and the goods they produced, but that the notion of actually owning the *person*, a person with a soul and a calling, would have been unthinkable to me.

Is that really how I would have felt? There's no way to know. What I do know is that most folks in the dominant white culture of that time and place did seem to feel like they *owned the person*. Many felt their religion reinforced this by teaching that we only enslave people who are *soul-less*, that slaves weren't *people* in the same way that free folks were *people*. That's always been a justification when humanity commits atrocities.

What about a land, a *place*? Can it have a soul of sorts?

I think the soul inside us longs to connect to the soul of a place. Maybe the nature of the soul is different among people and land, but it's there somehow. When a *people* are strongly connected as a tribe or a group or a community, they become connected to the soul of their *place*.

This gets to the nature of the misunderstanding between the Americans that lived here 300 years ago, and the Americans who came later. The Americans who were conquered didn't have the same notions of ownership of land that we do. They seemed confused by the concept of owning a *place*—maybe much like we'd be confused today by the notion of owning a person.

Waves of shimmering heat rise off the baking blacktop as I laboriously pedal, my unhappy stomach whining as the softened asphalt sucks at my tires. Every breath I take draws the heat into my lungs. The dark pavement absorbs the tyrannical heat of the July sun, radiating it back up to my feet and legs as they do their work closer to the ground. At this moment, I'm owned by the sun and the heat.

Looking off to my left toward a place about a mile away where I've spent many hours hunting deer, I see a broad-winged hawk coming toward me. I hear his cry, and it looks like something is wrapped around its head. A kingbird is riding on his head, and we watch an amazing rodeo unfold 30 feet above us as the hawk crosses the highway sporting a kingbird riding bareback on his shoulders.

The small bird disengages from the hawk, flying above it again for a few wingbeats, before descending again and landing on the hawk's shoulders. The hawk cries again while the smaller bird harasses it, riding its shoulders and head. For several more wingbeats the smaller bird hangs on, before disengaging and flying off again.

Cresting a hill, my hopes for a cool and breezy descent are dashed by level road and air that feels more like a blasting furnace than a cooling relief. My sweet tailwind is gone, the asphalt is so hot it's sucking my tires into the road, I'm hot, the lunch in my gut is angry at me, and I'm working harder than I think I should be working at this point.

I'm not feelin' the love.

A couple hundred yards ahead of me, Dave is suffering too. A pickup with a big horse trailer is coming in our direction, and I see him pull over to the side of the road. Dave rides over to the truck, chatting with the guy. I can't imagine the guy in the truck would be asking us for directions, and figure maybe he's just wanting to chat.

But something more simple and wonderful is happening. Once again, I'm about to experience the magic of genuine friendliness and heartfelt concern from another human being, one who doesn't know me from Adam.

As I catch up and pull over, the driver is just hopping back into his truck. He smiles and waves, pulling away as Dave hands me a bottle of ice cold water that the guy pulled out of his cooler. He wasn't looking to chat, or ask for anything. He just wanted to express a kindness in the form of cold water for a couple guys who looked like they could use it.

I don't remember many times in my life when I've had water this cold. I never stop pedaling, taking the bottle from Dave as he hands it to me and drinking it down while slowly riding there on the side of the road. The ice-cold liquid sucks some of the heat out of my insides as I pour it down my throat. The perfect elixir, meant for exactly this moment, delivered by an angel in cowboy boots and a cowboy hat, sporting a smile, a wave, and a heart of gold.

36

PIZZA DAVE

The real things haven't changed. It is still best to be honest and truthful; to make the most of what we have; to be happy with simple pleasures; and have courage when things go wrong.

Laura Ingalls Wilder

COLDWATER, KANSAS

Dave and I call it quits for the day in Coldwater. We've been hoping to push on to Medicine Lodge, but there's absolutely nothing along the 40 miles between Coldwater and Medicine Lodge. The heat took a lot out of us already today, and we don't really want to pick more of a fight with it than we're sure we can win. A shower and some rest in the air conditioning puts us right back together again, and we head down to the local diner for supper.

In Coldwater, the local diner is called Dave's Pizza Oven. It's a sparsely furnished converted old corner store that a fella named Dave has been running as a pizza place for several years now. While it doesn't fit the stereotype of the small-town diner, it serves the purpose quite nicely.

Folks in Coldwater seem to support Pizza Oven Dave as he maintains this last vestige of culture and community in this little town on the prairie. It's Sunday evening, and the place is jumping with locals. Everyone knows one another, and there's lots of meandering back and forth between tables, folks chatting and laughing and socializing, strengthening the bond of community that holds them together. The town is lucky to have someone like Dave, who's willing to put in the effort to be that place where the glue can flow.

Pizza Oven Dave comes over and chats with us for a while. He's an old (well, not as old as us) cyclist who worked at a bike shop up in Hays years ago. He moved his family here, and says raising a family and running the Pizza Oven doesn't leave him much time for cycling these days. I suspect that as time goes along, there'll be some cycling in Pizza Oven Dave's future again. Coldwater is lucky to have him. And the pizza's not bad either.

Pizza Oven Dave meanders back to the kitchen, and my Dave and I dive into some great discussion. We really enjoy the kind of discussion that would get us kicked out of casual encounters with other folks, stuff like religion and politics. This is important stuff, and Dave and I both feel strongly and passionately about many things. We might not always agree, but we think enough of each other to disagree with respect for the opinions of the other. At the end of the day, even when we don't agree, we usually find that the points of agreement dramatically outnumber the points of disagreement.

This evening, we're talking about joy in everyday life. Dave's pretty hard on himself, suggesting again that he misses out on quite a bit of the "joy of life" because he's so focused on the destination, so focused on checking things off his list. He views me as someone who's better at finding joy in the little things that happen along the journey.

Dave's pretty sure he doesn't have much "journey juice" in his veins. He's pretty sure he's missing out on lots of the joy that journey folks find along the way. I'm not buying the argument. There are surely joys that I find in the day that he misses, but I know there are joys that he finds along the way that are completely lost on me.

For example, Dave is a walking adding machine, able to recite at any moment exactly how many miles we've gone on the trip so far, and how many today, and how many to the next town with a motel. He keeps track of our mileage covered hour by hour, so in the middle of the day he can tell you exactly what our average speeds have been hour by hour throughout the day.

I usually don't even want to know this stuff, because it changes the complexion of the ride for me. But Dave finds joy in keeping track of this stuff and thinking about it as he rides. Real and true joy, I think. And what's wrong with that? Why is this joy any less meaningful than the joy I might find in the little things I see and discover along the path we're riding together? Is one manifestation of joy more "destination" focused than the other? Maybe. Maybe not. We each need to find the balance that works for us as we move along the path, and finding that balance opens us to recognize little moments along that path where joy might be waiting for us.

There are unexpected little joys along any path. By finding my balance, I can better see and accept the little moments of joy that a journey holds for me. By letting those little moments of joy infect my journey, I open myself to the magic along the path that might otherwise remain hidden. Allowing the journey to change me, and to define both me and the journey, reveals a greater destination than I could have envisioned.

Dave and I talk through these notions as we quell what little remaining appetite we have at the end of this day. We certainly don't end up knowing much more about the great questions of Life, The Universe, and Everything, but we're pretty sure the answer is 42. (*Thanks to Douglas Adams for that answer.*)

37

MEDICINE HILLS

The feeling remains that God is on the journey too.
Teresa of Avilan

DAY 20 • COLDWATER TO MEDICINE LODGE, KANSAS

Another morning, another convenience store in small-town America. A light breeze meanders up the road in the pre-dawn twilight. The early risers in town stop by to pick up their coffee and donuts as Dave and I wolf down liquid and calories. This has become our morning routine, and it feels both comfortable and comforting to me.

Today's section of road is one of the most beautiful places in America, and the only people who know about it are local folks who drive back and forth across southern Kansas. I've looked forward to this piece of the ride since we started planning, and I'm giddy with the anticipation of sharing this magical place with Dave.

It's a transitional land. You enter from the arid west through long rolling hills. By the time you leave Medicine Lodge headed east, the air is humid, the land is flat, and grazing land has been replaced by farmland.

These hills are known by several names. The road sign says "Gypsum Hills," named for the gypsum that's mined here. I've heard that the name given by the Americans who lived here 200 years ago translates to something like "Medicine Hills." For hundreds of generations, I suppose, the folks who lived here believed these hills were full of magic and medicine. Something integral to these hills was sacred and honored. The Medicine River flows from these hills, believed to carry curative powers.

How we name a place is a reflection of what we see in it, and it's interesting to look at the differences suggested in "Gypsum Hills" versus "Medicine Hills."

We give the name Gypsum Hills, because we take gypsum from the hills and haul if off to be used elsewhere. Gypsum is used to make wallboard, that material from which essentially all interior walls in our country are constructed. To the eyes of our culture today, the hills are a place where a mineral was left for us to take and use somewhere else.

To another people, the hills were named for the magic they felt when they were here. This place brought connection to their souls. After coming here, they must have felt enriched and enhanced. When they left, there was something they took with them, but it was spiritual richness rather than physical mineral. Perhaps they left something of themselves behind as well. Rather than taking something away from the hills, they brought themselves to the hills, and became something larger as a result. Nothing was taken. It was a symbiotic—maybe even synergistic—relationship, an ability to grow and gain without taking anything away.

In the first case, we find a thing and we take it, we haul it off in trucks and use it for the things we're building elsewhere. In the second case, the *place* gives a thing to us, but the place isn't depleted as a result. One is *taking*, the other *sharing*. One is redistributing a *resource*, the other worshiping a *place*.

I'm not suggesting it's evil to mine gypsum from the hills. I think our culture depends on materials like gypsum to continue to build the world we're building. I don't think this makes us evil. I'm only observing a difference in how *place* is perceived by us today, and how it seems to have been perceived by the Americans who were here before we were.

Whenever I'm here, I feel magic and medicine. I feel as though I'm receiving a gift. Out of respect for the magic in this wonderful little slice of Creation, I call it the Medicine Hills.

The first 20 miles or so this morning is terrain much like we rode through yesterday, rolling hills of green grass and rocky outcroppings. Many small spring-fed ponds dot the area. Traffic remains light, as it's been all across US 160.

The hills open up as we move further into them, becoming deeper and wider. Rises and peaks in the distance have a volcanic look to them. The early morning light reflecting on red clay paints crimson flames across the earth as far as we can see.

Usually when we're in hills, Dave passes me as we go up the hill, and then I pass him on the descent. I outweigh Dave by about 20 pounds, and these pounds manifest themselves very predictably in my slower ascents and faster descents. At the bottom of an early descent, my legs are feeling strong and spunky, so I lean into the effort and power up the hill. Reaching the top, I see Dave is still quite a ways behind. With another descent approaching, I let my body set the pace it likes, while my heart and mind enjoy the magic unfolding around me.

This is an unusual order of things, me out in front like this. Dave's greater strength and my greater frequency of stops generally translates to Dave waiting for me up the road. What's changing the pattern this morning? I stop to take some pictures, waiting as Dave catches up. As he pulls up beside me, I can tell he's working hard, not looking like he's hanging back and relaxing. I seem to be setting a pace he's good with.

Wow. What's up with this?

We start rolling again and I pull away, opening a nice gap between us. I feel strong and vibrant. My legs feel invincible. My lungs suck in volumes of the clean air, and my heart pounds with a magical rhythm.

Life is good. Really good.

A sweet moment of harmony between a body that's hitting its stride and a spirit filled with the goodness of the place it's riding through. Good Medicine is raining down on me, and few things in life can possibly feel this perfect.

I recognize something else in play as well. The ego. It *feels good* to be out in front. The feel good I'm getting from the ego gets thrown in with the nice harmony of body and spirit and the wonderful endorphins coursing through my body. The world is my oyster.

This ego effect is interesting stuff. It's a bit of a chicken and egg thing, in that I feel better when I'm in front, but I'm also more likely to be in front if I feel better. When my kids were little and we hiked together, I always tried to find a way to let them lead the way. If they were following, the pace was slower and the complaining spirit rose easily in them. Put them in front, let them set the pace, and they always set a significantly faster one.

When I'm in front and setting the pace, I feel a sense of responsibility, that someone behind me is depending on me to set a good pace. Being in front invigorates, making me feel like I need to keep the pace high or I'll get caught. Being in back makes me wonder if I'm holding people back. Being consistently in back is discouraging, as I'm constantly reminded that I'm not as strong as the guy who's consistently in front.

It's not that I consciously think these thoughts, but I think this is the subsurface chatter that's happening and defining my emotion.

How universal is this phenomenon? I wonder if the opposite happens with some people, depending on personality? How much does chatter differ between people? What about folks who would be bothered by the things I like, and who like the things that bother me? Does their chatter make them feel the opposite? Do they not perform as well when they're leading the way rather than following?

Do I feel good and strong in spirit because I'm in these hills this morning, which translates to physical well-being and strength, which puts me in front, which makes me feel good? Or was there some other order to what happened? Synchronicity. A good day came into being because these things came together in the right proportions at the right time.

Magic.

Good medicine.

38

MAGIC

We are all the children of God. The sun, the darkness,
the winds are all listening to what we have to say.

Geronimo

GOOD MEDICINE

We pull out into a scenic overlook at the top of a hill. After all the great scenery we've been immersed in over the last 20 miles or so, I figure this one must be really spectacular! The view is disappointing, not nearly as good as much of the view we've been moving through. Dave comments that if you were in a car, you wouldn't have been moving through it as slowly as we were, and you wouldn't have been stopping so often on the road to take pictures, so this spot where you could pull the car off the road, stop and take pictures, would feel like a really good spot.

Balance. In this case the balance between speed and intimacy. Moving more slowly down the highway facilitates a greater intimacy with the world we're moving through.

The sounds beside the road wrap our ears in the music of the place, and the wind across our faces drenches us in the smell of the place. Whenever we see a windmill or a pond that strikes us as particularly nice, we stop and enjoy it, maybe take a picture of it.

Many years ago, as a young man hiking in the northern Georgia mountains on the Appalachian Trail with my friend Scott Stuckey, I had a similar experience. I'd had a really beautiful day hiking, and at the end of the day, the trail descended a long ridge to a low spot. Here Scott and I crossed a highway, where folks had pulled their cars off to the side and were taking pictures. It struck me that our *low spot* for that afternoon, the place where the nice views and wilderness had been interrupted by this highway, was the *high spot* for the people driving cars on the highway. This was as good as it was going to get for them. This was their best experience of these wonderful mountains. I couldn't wait to get across the road and start climbing away from this low spot, while they wanted to spend as much time as they could soaking in this high point.

Perspective.

Looking out across the view from this pullout, I'm sure there are even better ways to experience the real depth of a place like the Medicine Hills, but it's plain to me just how well the bicycle does the trick. I'm happy to be on two wheels this morning.

Back in the saddle, we continue toward Medicine Lodge. I feel in perfect balance with my bicycle this morning. Days like today are what keep me coming back to the bicycle over and over, that harmony with tool or machine that can happen now and then.

For guys my age, it's like baseball. I grew up playing baseball. Lots of baseball. In the summer, a common pastime was to play catch. Two or three of us would stand in a yard or a field or a street, and throw the baseball back and forth. For hours. We'd make up games to go along with the throwing, playing out fantasies as we went, but it was really the throwing and catching of the ball that we loved.

When my dad taught me to throw and catch a baseball, I remember him telling me patiently and repeatedly that I'd eventually get to the place where instinct did all the work, where my mind didn't think about it, and my body didn't worry about it.

"It'll happen," he'd say as we threw the ball back and forth.

And it did. I have no idea when it happened, but it did. That sweet harmony between my body, the glove, and the ball. Hearing the satisfying snap as the ball pops into the sweet spot in the glove over and over. Wrapping my hand around the ball, feeling the laces exactly where they need to be. Hearing the spin of the ball through the air as it whips from my hand.

When I was about 12, I saved up and bought a really nice glove. I've still got that old ball glove. I've kept it oiled through the years, always with a ball resting in the pocket to maintain the right shape. I've gotten rid of lots of stuff over the years, but I've never parted with that glove. When my brother and I get together to fish in the summer, we always bring our ball gloves and play catch.

It's a spiritual experience for me.

The magic starts as I slip my hand into that old glove. The glove welcomes my hand like I might welcome a dear old friend I hadn't seen in too many years. The smell of the worn leather, the look of it, the weight of it in my hand.

Feeling the ball rest perfectly in my hand, laces fitting exactly beneath my fingertips. The weight of it rolling precisely off my fingertips as I throw it. The beautiful arc of it as it seeks the spot 20 yards away where my mind wants it to go.

Harmony.

The joy I feel in the melding of human and tool probably has an evolutionary advantage, as it makes us more effective users of tools. Our mind/body coordination adapts to the exact dimensions and weight and shape of the thing we're using. The thing becomes wired into us, part of us, almost like an arm or a leg is part of us. Our mind develops an attachment to the thing, much like it would to an arm or a leg. At some deep level, the *thing* becomes a part of *me*, and I have a deep joy at *being one with* the thing.

This morning, pedaling along this wonderful highway on a glorious Kansas morning, I'm feeling that deep joy. The light and responsive bicycle beneath me is a part of me. Like a worn and familiar baseball glove slipping on to my hand to play catch with my brother, the light and responsive bicycle beneath me feels right, a part of me.

Sweeping down a smooth asphalt ribbon into Medicine Lodge, we drop onto the small, lush flood plain of the Medicine River. We're disappointed that there doesn't appear to be a diner in town, so settle for truck stop breakfast again. Chicken fried steak of course, accompanied by jovial conversation with a couple of truckers.

We walk out of the restaurant in the company of a couple of bikers (the loud kind of bikes), talking about the roads east of here and the trip we have in front of us. We saddle up and start pedaling before they do, and we're a couple miles down the road by the time they catch up to us. They ride along beside us for a while, chatting over the clatter of their motors, trading good natured jabs. They wave as they let the horses in those big engines rev up, raising their arms in a wave of goodbye and solidarity as they fly off up the road, leaving Dave and I pedaling east into the haze of a beautiful Kansas morning as it progresses toward a humid July swelter.

We've reached the halfway point in our sojourn across the country. Behind us the western half of our journey blooms with memories growing sweeter with time. Ahead of us the promise of adventure beckons with open arms, the sweetness of anticipation ripe in the pilgrim's hope.

EPILOGUE

Wandering re-established the original harmony
which once existed between man and universe.

Anatole France

Medicine Lodge seems a perfect stopping point for this story. Rolling into the humid farmland east of Medicine Lodge, the texture of the places ahead of us would clearly be different from what was behind us. The ride continued, and the ride through the eastern half of the country becomes the next story. It's coincidence that Medicine Lodge is at the halfway point in terms of miles, since the real division of story comes from the change in the character of the land and the ride that happens there.

The sweetness of that morning ride into Medicine Lodge is something I remember well as I type these words — an exclamation point to a journey which was packed with sweet moments and lush memories, along with a little pain now and again. Writing about these memories and moments nourishes my anticipation for writing the rest of the story, the story of the completion of the ride to Annapolis.

•

Anticipation. Such a lonely word any more. In our quest for instant gratification, we sometimes lose touch with the sweetness of anticipation. We think longing is a bad thing, that longing implies that we don't have something we want. When we instantly get the thing we think we want, we can't figure out why having it feels so hollow. It's the longing we miss. The anticipation. The flirting.

Telling the story of yesterday helps us define the palette for our next adventure. It's how we learn to flirt with tomorrow. And in the flirting, we discover the true gift in the story we tell.

The one who tells the stories rules the world.

Hopi proverb